Albert Shaw Lectures on Diplomatic History

THE LIBERALITY OF ALBERT SHAW,
Ph.D. 1884, has made it possible for The Johns
Hopkins University to provide an annual course of
lectures on diplomatic history. This volume
contains the lectures delivered in 1954.

Albert Shaw Lectures on Diplomatic History

1899. *John H. Latané*. The Diplomatic Relations of the United States and Spanish America. 1900. (Out of print.)

1900. *James Morton Callahan*. The Diplomatic History of the Southern Confederacy. 1901. (Out of print.)

1906. *Jesse Siddall Reeves*. American Diplomacy under Tyler and Polk. 1907. $1.75.

1907. *Elbert Jay Benton*. International Law and Diplomacy of the Spanish-American War. 1908. $1.75.

1909. *Ephraim Douglass Adams*. British Interests and Activities in Texas, 1838–1846. 1910. (Out of print.)

1911. *Charles Oscar Paullin*. Diplomatic Negotiations of American Naval Officers, 1778–1883. 1912. $2.25.

1912. *Isaac J. Cox*. The West Florida Controversy, 1798–1813. 1918. $3.00.

1913. *William R. Manning*. Early Diplomatic Relations between the United States and Mexico. 1916. $2.50.

1914. *Frank A. Updyke*. The Diplomacy of the War of 1812. 1915. (Out of print.)

1917. *Payson Jackson Treat*. The Early Diplomatic Relations between the United States and Japan, 1853–1865. 1917. $2.75.

1921. *Percy Alvin Martin*. Latin America and the War. 1925. $3.50.

1923. *Henry Merritt Wriston*. Executive Agents in American Foreign Relations. 1929. $5.00.

1926. *Samuel Flagg Bemis*. Pinckney's Treaty: A Study of America's Advantage from Europe's Distress, 1783–1800. 1926. Second printing 1941. $3.00.

1927. *Bruce Williams*. State Security and the League of Nations. 1927. $2.75.

1928. *J. Fred Rippy*. Rivalry of the United States and Great Britain over Latin America, 1808–1830. 1929. (Out of print.)

1930. *Victor Andrés Belaunde*. Bolivar and the Political Thought of the Spanish American Revolution. 1938. $3.50.

1931. *Charles Callan Tansill*. The Purchase of the Danish West Indies. 1932. $3.50.

1932. *Dexter Perkins*. The Monroe Doctrine, 1826–1867. 1933. (Out of print.)

1933. *Charles Seymour*. American Diplomacy during the World War. 1934. Second printing 1942. $3.00.

1935. *Frank H. Simonds*. American Foreign Policy in the Post-war Years. 1935. $2.00.

1936. *Julius W. Pratt*. Expansionists of 1898: The Acquisition of Hawaii and the Spanish Islands. 1936. (Out of print.)

1937. *Dexter Perkins*. The Monroe Doctrine, 1867-1907. 1937. $3.50.

1938. *Arthur Preston Whitaker*. The United States and the Independence of Latin America, 1800–1830. 1941. (Out of print.)

1939. *William Spence Robertson*. France and Latin-American Independence. 1939. $3.75.

1941. *Thomas A. Bailey*. The Policy of the United States toward the Neutrals, 1917–1918. 1942. $3.50.

1942. *Wilfrid Hardy Callcott*. The Caribbean Policy of the United States, 1890–1920. 1943. $3.50.

1946. *Malbone W. Graham*. American Diplomacy in the International Community. 1949. $3.25.

1950. *Herbert Feis*. The Diplomacy of the Dollar, First Era, 1919–1932. 1950. $2.25.

1951. *Edward Hallett Carr*. German-Soviet Relations between the Two World Wars, 1919–1939. 1951. $3.00.

1954. *Max Beloff*. Foreign Policy and the Democratic Process. 1955. $3.00.

Foreign Policy and the Democratic Process

The Albert Shaw Lectures

ON DIPLOMATIC HISTORY, 1954

F OREIGN POLICY

and the Democratic Process

BY MAX BELOFF, *Nuffield Reader in the
Comparative Study of Institutions at the University of Oxford
and Fellow of Nuffield College, Oxford*

BALTIMORE   *The Johns Hopkins Press*   1955

Distributed in Great Britain by
Geoffrey Cumberlege: Oxford University Press, London

Printed in U.S.A. by The William Byrd Press, Richmond

Library of Congress Catalog Card No. 55-9743

Preface

Iₙ publishing these lectures delivered in November 1954, I must acknowledge a five-fold indebtedness: to
The Johns Hopkins University where the lectures were delivered,
to the Institute for Advanced Study, Princeton, where they were
written, to the Firestone Library of Princeton University whose
resources were indispensable, to my own University and College
for a term's leave of absence, and to the Rockefeller Foundation
which for the second time enabled me to spend such a term in
travel and study in the United States.

My debt to other writers in this field is I hope adequately
demonstrated in the notes; I am obliged to their publishers for
permission to quote from a number of copyright works named
there. I have also had much direct information from individuals
many of whom are now or were previously in the service of the
United States government. It would be a poor reward for their
generosity to name them individually in a preface to so contro-
versial a book. They will know that this silence does not signify
any lack of gratitude, or of renewed awareness of the ready help-
fulness of Americans to all students of their country.

One student of foreign policy now no longer with us may be
mentioned with impunity; I do not know whether the late Edward
Mead Earle would have subscribed to everything in these lectures:
I like to think that he, who did so much to foster Anglo-American
historical studies, would have found them a not inappropriate
though incomplete return for the privilege of an invitation to the
Institute for Advanced Study, extended to me on his initiative.

PRINCETON, NEW JERSEY   *Max Beloff*
   MAY 1955

Contents

I *The Problem*
OF DEMOCRATIC FOREIGN POLICY

THE FOREIGN STUDENT OF THE AMERICAN SCENE
in the middle years of the twentieth century is bound to regard
as one of its salient features the extent to which fundamental
questions of national policy have become the subject of
sustained and serious debate. When all allowances are made
for the vigor of political partisanship—and no student
would be worthy of the name who could not make these allowances—it remains clear that this debate reflects something
deeper than the tussles for power of competing sectional interests within the nation, or of their professional representatives on the political scene. In as far as the internal aspect
of the nation's affairs is concerned, the European observer
may find the extent of agreement more remarkable than the
number of marginal cases which still afford room for dispute.
In the quarter of a century that has elapsed since the onset
of the great depression, the devotion of the United States to
a capitalistic economy tempered by state intervention prag-
matically conceived, and to its traditional representative
institutions, in the sphere of politics, would seem to have
been, if anything, strengthened by the developments that have
taken place. The widespread rejection even in non-Communist
Europe of the traditional role of property, the widespread
questioning of the ability of representative institutions to
handle the economic and social problems of modern society
find in this country only the remotest of echoes.

It is indeed more than likely that such an observer will be
struck not by the extent to which such revolutionary or radical ideas are held as by the apparent alarm which they inspire
in a people so obviously and understandably immune to their

seductions. It is important that he should not overestimate either the novelty or the extent of this reaction against unorthodox and unpopular ideas. The identification of a tenderness about civil rights with devotion to the democratic principle is commonly made by American intellectuals, though it has little obvious warrant either in history or in logic. The dominant faction in the community will try to make intellectuals respect its prejudices—as was clear for instance at the time of the 1896 election. An ideal polity might embody a synthesis of liberalism and democracy but, in an imperfect world, a society based on the idea of popular rule is more likely to respect conformity than the reverse. This does not however provide a full explanation of the contemporary paradox.

The clue to the internal tension in American affairs is surely to be found in the fact that what is really at issue is not the future of an American society conceived of as following its own autonomous pattern of development. It is the impact upon this society of external events. The essential quality of the ideas that are considered so dangerous as to warrant stern measures of both legal and extra-legal repression is to be found in the fact that their source is an alien one. What they call into question is not the relationship between one group of Americans and another, as has been true of many past movements that have successfully been assimilated into the central national tradition, but the relationship between American society as a whole and the external world. The core of the current American debate is to be found in the argument over foreign not domestic policy, or rather in the zone where the two arguments meet.

3

If this interpretation be correct the situation is still not without its parallels in the American past. The first great political crisis of the new nation—that which culminated in the Alien and Sedition Acts—was the result of the impact upon the American scene, at a time when American foreign policy was still unformulated, of the passions excited by Revolutionary France. Indeed, since the lessons that George Washington drew from the effects of this impact have been given so permanent an embodiment in the Farewell Address, it would be permissible to regard this crisis as among the most durable of the conditioning factors in the nation's history. Again, although the Know-Nothing movement of the eighteen-fifties had no doubt a multiple explanation, it seems clear that insofar as its animus was directed against Roman Catholics, the reason was that the Papacy was regarded as in a sense a foreign power, adherence to whose religious tenets might mean something less than total national allegiance on the part of the church's American component. It is hardly necessary to do more than recall for the sake of completeness the way in which, during and after the First World War, the American involvement overseas was reflected in an almost unbridled concern for political conformity at home, and in admitted excesses in enforcing it.

It is true of course that in the modern world no social or political movement anywhere can be altogether without international repercussions. Even the agrarian populism of the eighteen-nineties, an apparently autonomous outgrowth of the local circumstances of the American prairies, developed through its concern with monetary factors a distinctive and important attitude of its own towards foreign policy, based upon the alleged iniquities of the London money market. But such issues could be, and were, fought out with neither side obviously impinging or intending to impinge upon America's power to control her own destinies. Neither side in the great political contest of 1896 could seriously be accused of seeking for inspiration outside a national tradition varied enough to accommodate them both. Nor forty years later were things very different. The American opponents of the New Deal might use its alleged intellectual indebtedness to European socialism as a weapon of political controversy; the identification was too patently artificial for the charge to stick. There is a very real difference between such situations and those where a minority is under attack because it represents the power of an external, alien and hostile society.[1]

For the clearest example of what happens in such a situation, one would have to go to the history not of the American people but of a segment of it—to the history of the ante bellum South. There we find a society possessed of a strong liberal tradition gradually finding itself constrained to repudiate this heritage and to insist upon universal acquiescence in the existence and protection of the institution which it regarded as fundamental to its social order. Neither the political platform, nor the pulpit nor the professorial lectern might safely be used to disseminate the contrary doctrine. The mails were censored to prevent the circulation of abolitionist literature. After the John Brown raid in 1859 these

---

[1] On efforts at enforcing conformity in the populist period and later, see Eric Goldman, *Rendezvous with Destiny* (New York, Knopf, 1952).

fears became concrete in the belief that the Northern fanatics were planning a slave revolt. "Out of this jittery state of mind or popular hysteria" writes a recent and not unsympathetic historian of the old South "arose numerous vigilance committees to ferret out the emissaries of servile insurrection. As a result, Northern travelers, schoolteachers, peddlers, and workmen in the South were in constant danger of being brought before vigilance committees, flogged, and expelled from the country on the basis of unfounded suspicions."[2] These and other manifestations of Southern apprehension, down to the final tragedy of Secession itself, were not the product of fears about the internal cohesion and stability of Southern society. The traditional wielders of economic, social and political power in that region were not obviously threatened by the mass of non-slaveholding whites, still less by the slaves. The menace as they saw it came from outside the South, from the growth on their borders of a rival social order, continually expanding in wealth and might and dedicated, as they believed, to the eradication of the cherished Southern way of life. In the face of this menace, the closing of the ranks seemed but elementary prudence; nor has this instinctive reaction been without significance in more recent decades of Southern history.[3]

As is the case with most historical parallels, this is a very imperfect one. What gave cogency to the Southern case be-

---

[2] Clement Eaton, *A History of the Southern Confederacy* (New York, Macmillan, 1954), p. 2.

[3] See W. J. Cash, *The Mind of the South* (New York, Knopf, 1941).

fore the Civil War was not merely that the North, and indeed most of the civilized world, at the time, had categorically repudiated the ideological foundations of human slavery, but that the rival system of free labor was producing better results. The fundamental statistics both human and material were available to demonstrate the North's growing advantage. In the case of the challenge to the United States presented by Soviet Communism, the outside observer at any rate can find no such adverse disparity. He is, however, bound to conclude that his view is by no means universally shared among Americans. Whatever their inner convictions may be, many Americans write, and some act, as though they formed a beleaguered garrison around whose crumbling ramparts the enemy were assembling in ever greater strength.

Some American discussion on these momentous matters goes so far as to give the impression that the parallel is well founded, that Americans think that their freedoms are as endangered as was Southern slavery in the eighteen-fifties. And even where such ideas are repudiated as essentially morbid, the whole discussion on American foreign policy, and on the appropriate machinery for conducting it, is carried on with an intensity and a passion that should warn the foreigner against any rash attempt to intervene.

The foreigner may perhaps observe that the current debate on American foreign policy should not be studied and cannot be understood wholly in the light of the immediate challenge presented by Soviet Communism. It did not begin with this challenge; and it would not be wholly resolved, even if the challenge were suddenly to disappear. Its very language and the sides that people take upon disputed questions can only be understood in the light of rather more than fifty years of American responses to a changing international scene. It is no accident that the most significant contribution to the debate so far should open with a consideration of the Spanish-American War.[4] Not that it was that war that made the United States a great power; rather, it was the occasion for the recognition of that status by foreigners and, still more important, by Americans themselves.[5] And what has been debated since then are the implications of this fact and of other momentous developments in the world both for American policy and for the American domestic institutions, upon which that policy rests, and for the preservation of which it presumably exists.

The Soviet challenge has only stimulated awareness of the extent of the changes that have taken place both in America itself and in its external environment. One might have expected some equal awareness and possibly some similar self-searchings in other countries whose place in the world has altered no less drastically than America's. The international scene studied by diplomatic historians concerned with the late nineteenth century consisted of a world of some seven or eight great powers of which all but two were wholly or essentially European. During the period since the Second World War we have been taught to view things in the light of the rivalry between two powers and two powers only; the United States,

---

[4] George F. Kennan, *American Diplomacy, 1900–1950* (University of Chicago Press, 1951).

[5] Cf. E. M. Earle, "A Half-Century of American Foreign Policy," *Political Science Quarterly* (June, 1949).

a wholly non-European power, and the Soviet Union, a power which if still essentially European, comprises a strong Asiatic component. It may be correct to assume, as do some authorities, that this particular phase has been only a passing one, and that "bipolarity," as it is called, is ceasing to represent international realities.[6] It is certainly the case that the nineteenth-century state of affairs is hardly likely to reemerge. And yet a country like Great Britain, whose role has been altered as much as anyone's by these shifts in world power, appears, on the surface at least, much less prone to call into question either the policies she has actually followed or the traditional methods used to arrive at them.

Two suggestions may be offered as to why the discussion should have taken a sharper turn in the United States. In the first place it seems obvious to the foreign observer that Americans have taken much more closely to heart the impact upon international relations in general of the new powers of destruction now available to man. It is not simply that there is greater consciousness of what such things can mean in terms of actual warfare. Americans have not got over, may perhaps never quite get over, the shock to their consciences that it should have fallen to them—to a nation dedicated to peaceful and humanitarian ideals—to make the transition to the era of atomic destructiveness. It would have been logical for the initiative to have been taken by some great militaristic nation—the Germans or the Japanese; it was ironic that the fatal signal should have been given by the

---

[6] George F. Kennan, *Realities of American Foreign Policy* (Princeton University Press, 1954), p. 100.

representative of an essentially civilian-minded people, by someone so unlike the prototype of the ruthless military dictator as President Harry Truman.

But this is not the whole story; what Americans also appear to have come to see is that the very existence of power of this particular kind, a power based upon technological achievement, may make it impossible for them to retain in their own hands and to exercise by normal procedures those rights which have been the very heart of their being as a democratic community. Perhaps because they are more familiar with the idea of scientific progress than are members of communities where technological strides have been less dramatic as the causes of social change, perhaps simply because their imagination has been less blunted by the actual experience of evil and less harnessed by the acceptance of routine responses, Americans have been more alive to the novelty of the problem without indeed claiming that they possess the key to its solution. They at least suspect that at last human power may really have outgrown the capacities of social institutions, seeing that these can hardly transcend the fallible human beings who have to make them work. They face, with some inkling at least of what it may imply, what one American historian has recently called "this new world where science and policy intersect at the point of maximum destructiveness; where the life and death of civilization may hang on incomprehensible equations fed into giant calculating machines; where yet the old human emotions—love, loyalty, envy, hate —are still alive and powerful."[7]

---

[7] Arthur M. Schlesinger, Jr., "The Oppenheimer Case," *Atlantic Monthly* (October, 1954).

The second reason why the debate has taken on so strident a tone in America may relate to something deriving more specifically from America's own experience. It would be the fact that the element of disillusion and frustration which bulks so large in the world outlook of contemporary Americans is still so novel as to be almost unassimilable. A history of American diplomacy published in 1915 could still include a final chapter entitled, with no trace of irony: "Success and Its Causes." "Our diplomacy," it begins, "has, on the whole, served the national needs and purposes exceptionally well." It was probably true, its author agreed, that the growth of democracy had made diplomacy more difficult in most countries; "the reverse has been true in the United States."[8]

This view was, in 1915, not at all farfetched; given the limited objectives that the United States had sought, its past success was undeniable. Provided that, as the author thought possible, such limited objectives were adequate for the future, there was no reason to doubt that success also lay ahead. It is understandable how difficult it must have been for a people believing that it could command success to find how far removed from reality such beliefs might prove to be. On two successive occasions the soaring idealism of wartime presidents and of many of the more active and vocal elements of the nation has had to give way to the grayer mood of everyday bargaining, and to the consciousness of new threats to peace and security. If the aftermath of World War I seemed to involve a failure to spread American ideals further abroad,

---

[8] C. R. Fish, *American Diplomacy* (New York, Henry Holt, 1915), pp. 497–99.

the aftermath of World War II revealed an apparent threat to these ideals even at home. Nor can these events be regarded as simply a series of misfortunes or mistakes. Only a petty mind can see in the history of a great nation nothing but ineptitudes and treacheries. There is no need to ascribe to President Wilson or to President Roosevelt more than their normal share of human fallibility, for in nearly all the major decisions that they made they took good care to see that they did not outstrip the common opinion; the nation as a whole is concerned in their reputations. But to say this is only to transfer the discussion onto another plane; for, if the policies that the United States has followed have been wholly or partially erroneous, and if these policies have been formulated through constitutional processes by the nation's accredited leaders, and implemented by constitutional means, then the argument must necessarily turn inwards and begin to discuss whether the traditional political equipment of the community is adequate for the tasks it is now forced to confront.

Once this shift in emphasis takes place, once the debate becomes not a debate about policy but a debate about how policies were or should have been arrived at, it cannot long confine itself to simple questions of the appropriate mechanisms; it is bound to continue to probe until it calls into question the most fundamental of all American beliefs: that of the absolute validity of the American philosophy of government and of the institutions in which it has become embodied. This is not something that lends itself to light treatment; it can hardly avoid stirring the most violent national feelings. And these feelings, though national in expression, are not

12

essentially national in content; to challenge democracy in America means to challenge it universally.

It could hardly be otherwise; and to say this is by no means to suggest that Americans are peculiarly egocentric or particularly given to national self-satisfaction. The characteristic feature of the American attitude to politics has always been its universalism. This is true even of the isolationist strain in the American tradition—for the point of historic isolationism is that it was an attempt to preserve for mankind those particular virtues and achievements of Americans which foreign involvements would tarnish or imperil. The concept of a peculiar racial destiny, which has tempted other peoples, has never—and for obvious reasons—carried full conviction in America, though it has had its own echoes on the American scene. The idea of a special geographical providence has had a better run and still underlies much popular American feeling about foreign affairs, even if it is now dismissed in more informed quarters. The dominant element has been what could reasonably be described, after the Jeffersonian and Jacksonian postscripts to the original Revolution, as a conscious, national self-dedication to the democratic principle. Not merely has America been the classic country of democracy; but democracy's potentialities have been assessed generally in American terms.

For a century and more, the Americans have primarily been occupied with trying to find solutions for internal problems which have appeared to threaten the validity of the central principle of their polity. The first of these—the contradiction presented by the existence in their midst of human slavery— was decided in its essentials by the outcome of the Civil War.

13

Yet the surviving question of how to create the necessary conditions for a multiracial society, with its different elements coexisting on a basis of political and social equality, still calls for the energies of some of the nation's best minds, and for all, perhaps, of the nation's best qualities. The second challenge was that presented by the accumulation within American society, particularly after the Civil War, of immense personal and corporate fortunes and the seeming use of such fortunes to corrupt and overawe the processes of government on the local and even the national scale. Again the field was, and remains, one big enough for the endeavors of whole generations to be occupied in discovering and implementing the appropriate remedies.

The new challenge, that of finding the best method of handling the nation's foreign relations, and as a corollary, and an important one, that of finding a proper place for the vast military establishments which these relations have come to involve, can only properly be estimated if it is seen in relation to these preceding ones. For it is essential to understand why it was that those most devoted to internal reform should most have resented what appeared to them as a diversion of interest and of resources to foreign goals and, in the last resort, to war. The common European picture of the American isolationist as an exponent of reactionary policies at home and abroad is colored by the natural European desire to feel assured of American support, and by the inevitable transformation of that desire into an assumption that it is America's duty as well as her interest to intervene positively in Europe's affairs.

There are no doubt groups on the present-day American

scene who fit this European stereotype; but this does not detract from the fact that the competition for human and material resources between domestic welfare and national security is a recurrent feature in the history of most countries; it undoubtedly underlies some of the shifts even in Soviet policy. Insofar as the argument for American isolationism has been (as it largely was until 1940) that the adoption of different and more passive policies would have assisted America to avoid facing this dilemma, it is difficult to withhold from it at least a measure of sympathy. Indeed, if one remembers how deeply rooted in the minds of the nation's founders was the desire to withdraw from the cycle of Europe's wars and how large military conscription bulked in the picture of the Old World retained by later generations of immigrants into the New, one can understand how close has been the relationship on American soil between pacifism and some aspects of the democratic ideal.[9] From one point of view, the candidacy of Henry Wallace for the presidency, in 1948, may have marked the final debacle of this alliance.

It was not merely the selfish and the materialistically inclined who resented the impact of the new demands made upon America by the world outside; the new situation was a shock to idealists as well. Both world wars came upon the country at a time when reformers and idealists were in the ascendancy, domestically speaking, and the country's reactions took a considerable coloring from their approach.

---

[9] On the connection between isolationism and progressivism, see Eric Goldman, *Rendezvous with Destiny*, especially pp. 234, 246, 264, 275, 282, 375.

The history of American foreign relations in the last half-century has been dealt with by some writers as largely a story of idealistic self-deception.[10] Other treatments regard the moral urges of American society itself as too integral a part of the whole to be thus rudely dismissed; but in any event, tension between ideals and self-interest, if one is to use this particular terminology, is such that it cannot be set aside.[11] Indeed, the development of a similar discussion in Great Britain was perhaps only interrupted by the coming of war in 1939.[12]

The difficulty is that those who take part in discussions conducted along these lines tend to find themselves neglecting the ways in which such tensions are in fact resolved within particular political systems. The historian is always aware, of course, of the measure of ambiguity involved. ". . . the attribution of thought and behaviour to nations," writes an American authority "is simply a convenient manner of speaking about significant ways in which large numbers of individual citizens think about their nation with respect to other nations." It is not a question of some mystical group-person but of the fact that the citizen does in reality orient "himself to his national environment by identifying himself with his nation-state and projecting upon this personified group of

[10] See, for example, Hans J. Morgenthau, *In Defense of the National Interest* (New York, Knopf, 1951).

[11] See, for example, Robert Endicott Osgood, *Ideals and Self-Interest in America's Foreign Relations* (University of Chicago Press, 1953).

[12] See E. H. Carr, *The Twenty Years Crisis* (London, Macmillan, 1939).

individuals his own thoughts and emotions."[13]

This is of course a perfectly legitimate manner of speech so long as all the members of the particular community concerned are affected by similar tides of feeling and respond in the same way to similar impulses. But such generalized impulses, though vitally important when they occur—as witness the general hardening of the British attitude towards Nazi Germany after March, 1939—are not the stuff of which foreign policy is normally made. This is true even if we leave out of account those societies in which a deep inner schism leads an appreciable body of the citizenry to identify itself with the fortunes of a foreign state rather than those of its own, as has been the case with the proletariats of France and Italy since the Second World War. For all modern societies are made up of a variegated set of social groups which may differ sharply about external policy and whose divergences may indeed be so great that statesmanship is left with little to build upon. It is often assumed that this is true only of democracies; but one suspects that similar contradictions in interest and outlook exist almost universally, and that totalitarianism serves to conceal rather than to suppress them. The evidence of the Nuremberg and still more of the Tokyo war-criminals' trials is emphatic in this respect.[14] Furthermore, it is well to keep in mind that the

---

[13] Robert E. Osgood, *Ideals and Self-Interest in America's Foreign Relations*, p. 3.

[14] On the divergences over foreign policy within the Japanese state structure, see F. C. Jones, *Japan's New Order in East Asia, 1937–45* (London, Oxford, 1954).

amount of attention any groups other than those profession-
ally concerned will devote to foreign policy is itself a variable;
the election campaign of 1954 in the United States went some
way toward suggesting to an observer that the debate on
foreign policy might find a temporary resolution through a
simple loss of interest on the part of the electorate.

If such considerations apply, then it is clear that the only
meaning that can be attached to a phrase like the "national
attitude" or the "national policy" will be that which is formulated by the constituted organs of its government and enforced by those elements of the nation's power which those
organs have at their disposal. And this will be equally true
whether the policy be one of idealism or of self-interest, or
some synthesis of the two.

In a full democracy this can be done only through the
accepted democratic processes. It is true that most democratic
political systems have made some differentiation between processes suitable for the formulation of foreign policy and those
appropriate for internal affairs. But until very recently,
particularly in America, it was above all in domestic affairs
that these processes were made use of, and the conventions for
their employment crystallized. The election of the appropriate
organs, their interrelationship, the nature and role of political
parties—all these have been geared to the solution of domestic
problems. To say that they have not done a good job in
America would be to deny the evidence of one's eyes. What is
now being questioned is whether these procedures are self-
evidently appropriate for the quite different kind of problems
which foreign policy presents, or may present. When a critic
writes, "the system under which we are going to have to con-

tinue to conduct foreign policy is, I hope and pray, the system of democracy,"[15] what he would seem to mean from the context is that he hopes that the United States can for its general purposes preserve a democratic system. But to judge from his criticism of previous American foreign policies and attitudes, this would seem to demand either a different set of attitudes to foreign affairs on the part of the American democracy, or certain institutional changes which would have the effect of limiting democracy with regard to at least some of its claims in this field. In a more recent work, the same authority writes, "to conduct foreign policy, means, at bottom, to shape the behavior of a nation wherever that behavior has impacts on its external environment. This is something only a government can do. For that reason, only a government can speak usefully and responsibly in foreign affairs."[16]

In making this and similar claims for the primacy of government, and in particular of the executive branch of government under the American system, this writer and those who think with him are suggesting the abandonment of certain political habits which have come to be associated with the conduct of foreign policy under a democratic system. It is important to note that, so far from meeting with universal support, such claims represent a point of view which is diametrically opposed to that held by other respected members of the community. A writer in the *American Political Science Review* tells us—the date is 1949—"the fact is that although we have gained publicity for foreign affairs and that is in

---

[15] George F. Kennan, *American Diplomacy*, p. 73.
[16] George F. Kennan, *Realities of American Foreign Policy*, p. 43.

itself important we have not democratized foreign affairs."[17]
And as we shall see much of the support that Congress can
muster in its claim for a greater share in the making of policy
derives from the belief that it is likely to be more responsive
to public opinion than the executive branch, and that an increase in its role would in itself be a gain for democracy in
this field.

The argument in this form naturally embodies certain
particular features deriving directly from the American
scene; but it is not specifically American in essentials. In
other countries also, and notably in Britain, there has been
at times a demand for greater democratization, for more
"popular" or "democratic" control of foreign policy, and
this has most usually taken the form of asking that Parliaments should have a greater voice in foreign affairs. In these
countries, and notably again in Britain, this argument has
come overwhelmingly from the political left; and has been
based on the presumption that a greater popular voice in the
conduct of foreign affairs would prevent governments from
making commitments likely to lead the country into war.

The first phase of the argument in Britain revolved around
the Labour and radical opposition to the increasing involvement of Britain in the European politics of the years before
the First World War, and in particular to the highly unpopular Entente with the reactionary Russian tsardom.[18]

---

[17] James Marshall, "Citizen Diplomacy," *American Political Science Review* (February, 1949).

[18] See Max Beloff, *Lucien Wolf and the Anglo-Russian Entente,
1907-14* (London, Jewish Historical Society of England, 1951).

Although the extent of Britain's commitments was not in fact known, the view of Sir Edward Grey's critics was that Parliament, which at that time rarely debated foreign affairs, ought to be given a greater say. The British Parliament and public were actually given less information at this time in the form of published diplomatic documents than their predecessors had had in the time of Palmerston. Furthermore, important figures in the Foreign Office and in the government deplored all public discussion of foreign policy—the latter because of the threat it presented to the unity of the Liberal party.[19] Although Grey had said in 1909 that in his view the House of Commons exercised a "more constant control" over foreign policy than was usual in foreign Parliaments,[20] the Government was sufficiently moved to secure from its embassies and legations abroad a series of reports on the practice in other countries which were laid before Parliament in 1912.[21] Lord Bryce, who presumably felt that his own views on American institutions hardly needed restatement, left the task, where the United States was concerned, to his Counsellor of Embassy, who after judicially comparing the role of Congress with that of Parliament tactfully concluded with the words: "each country can therefore advance solid reasons on behalf of its own system."

---

[19] A. J. P. Taylor, *The Struggle for Mastery in Europe, 1848–1918* (Oxford, Clarendon Press, 1954), pp. 526, 569–71.

[20] Speech of May 27, 1909, House of Commons *Debates*, 1909, vol. 5, Col. 1399.

[21] *Treatment of International Relations by Parliaments in European Countries, the United States and Japan* (Cmd. 6102, 1912, House of Commons Sessional Papers, 1912–13, vol. 68).

The Wilsonian doctrine of "open covenants openly arrived at," while not without its embarrassing aspects where British officialdom was concerned, fell on fertile soil in the Labour party, to which most of the old radical and near-pacifist wing of the Liberals now adhered, largely indeed just because of their attitude on foreign policy questions. The first British Labour Government secured another series of reports on foreign practice[22] and made known to the House of Commons that it was its intention during its term of office "to inform the House of all agreements, commitments, and understandings which may in any way bind the nation to specific action in certain circumstances."[23] The refusal of its Conservative successor to renew this pledge led to a House of Commons debate on the whole subject on March 11, 1925.[24]

The essential point of the resolution moved on behalf of the Labour party was that Parliament should be informed before any treaties or other diplomatic arrangements or understandings with foreign countries involving national obligations were concluded, and that no preparations for military co-operation with foreign countries consequent upon such understandings should be otherwise lawful. This argument arose of course, from the view taken of the circumstances under which Britain had gone to war in 1914. It was urged

---

[22] *Reports on the Methods adopted by Parliaments of Foreign Countries, for dealing with International Questions* (Cmd. 2282, 1924, House of Commons Sessional Papers, 1924–25, vol. 23).

[23] Statement by Arthur Ponsonby, Under-Secretary for Foreign Affairs, April 1, 1924, House of Commons *Debates*, 5th ser., vol. 171, Col. 1999–2006.

[24] *Ibid.*, vol. 181, Col. 1430–1474.

that Sir Edward Grey's claim that it had been sufficient to consult Parliament only in the final crisis was "a misinterpretation of democracy"; the Conservatives were warned that if they did not renew the Labour pledge about publicity, the Labour party might act by statute to confer the power of treaty-making itself upon Parliament.[25]

In replying for the Government, the Under-Secretary for Foreign Affairs restated the traditional British viewpoint.[26] The conduct of foreign affairs was an executive matter and could not be otherwise: "the Secretary of State for Foreign Affairs is an executive officer. You cannot deprive him of that position." The democratic element in the British system was that enshrined in the right of the House of Commons to dismiss a ministry with whose policies it disagreed, and ultimately in the dependence of the House itself upon the electorate. The member for Cambridge University learnedly supported this argument by pointing out the embarrassment that Congressional control was liable to cause to the United States government.[27] Although it has remained a legitimate political weapon for use against particular policies to claim that the voice of Parliament or of the "people" should be heard, the vote of 133 against 255 which the Labour motion received in the 1925 debate represents in some respects the high-water mark of the democratic protest where Britain is concerned. As its opponents were not slow to point out, the Labour Government had itself violated the spirit of the motion

---

[25] Speech of the Rt. Hon. C. P. Trevelyan.
[26] Speech of Ronald McNeill (later Lord Cushendun).
[27] Speech of Sir Geoffrey Butler.

in its handling of the Soviet treaty in the previous year; and subsequent Labour Governments seem to have been content to maintain undisturbed the existing procedures. There had of course been a change in that foreign affairs had meanwhile become (as they have remained) a much more important part of the Parliamentary diet than they had been during Grey's tenure of the Foreign Office; but this did not affect the essentials of the system.

The parallel American movement, as I have already indicated, would seem originally to have had much in common with its British counterpart. And this was undoubtedly true of much of the support for the neutrality legislation of the nineteen-thirties and for the proposed Ludlow Amendment. The comparison does not apply so aptly to some more recent manifestations of the demand for popular or Congressional control. The earlier view was that governments tended to be too warlike and to enter too easily into commitments which obliged their peoples to use force in their support. The newer view in America, deriving from one possible and much discussed interpretation of the diplomacy of the later Roosevelt and Truman periods, is that the executive's policy has proved too weak, too ready to indulge in what is sometimes called appeasement and that popular control is necessary as a "stiffener." When such issues become involved in party politics, additional complications arise. More people would agree that secrecy, particularly about military dispositions, is an important ingredient in a strong foreign policy; yet in 1951 it was President Truman's Congressional opponents who forced him to reveal the number of American divisions to be committed to Europe under the North Atlantic Treaty and, where the Far East was concerned, to disclose further "quantities of normally sacrosanct information about American political and strategic thinking."[28]

Without pursuing these points further at the moment, it is worthwhile calling attention to them because they illustrate what is one of the most baffling of all the problems that confront a student of the whole subject. The shape of institutions is rarely in itself a subject of concern except to the specialist. The clamor for change only comes to the fore when it is felt that the particular institutions have not been yielding the best results. And clearly this is as true of the foreign as of the domestic field. Those who in a sense want "more democracy" in foreign affairs, just as those who in a sense want "less democracy," do so because they are dissatisfied with what has been or is being done; they differ only as to the diagnosis and the cure.

Both sides have this in common: they accept the view that it is possible to find a proper place for the democratic principle in the field of foreign affairs and that there is no inherent incompatibility between democratic government, as such, and success in the sphere of external relations. In Britain, as we have seen, democratic control is largely limited to the ultimate sanction of cabinet responsibility; but it could be argued that the democratic nature of Britain's domestic government has itself no other sanction. In the United States, where the legislature plays a more immediate role in many aspects of government, and where it is itself more immediately

---

[28] R. P. Stebbins, *The United States in World Affairs, 1951* (New York, Harper and Bros., 1952), pp. 54–55, 104.

responsive to public opinion, its influence is more pervasive in foreign affairs just as it is in domestic legislation. And with the rise in the authority of the House of Representatives, which has been an inevitable consequence of the increasing dependence of American foreign policy upon the size and scope of financial appropriations, the attempted constitutional distinction between the two spheres has shown a marked tendency to contract.[29]

To someone who has to work the system—either system—the scope for directed change is obviously very small. He pays with caution for the possibilities of service. The external observer with no such responsibilities can afford to ask more radical questions and may feel that at least some of the confusion would be eliminated if historical experience elsewhere were drawn upon more freely. Is it possible that the whole search for a truly democratic foreign policy is based upon an illusion as to its possibility? Are there at least lessons that can be learned by discussing our experience in these terms? For the moment it may be well if I remind you of the opinion of a more qualified observer of the American scene:

> As for myself, I have no hesitation in avowing my conviction, that it is most especially in the conduct of foreign relations that democratic governments appear to me to be decidedly inferior to governments carried on upon different principles. Experience, instruction, and habit may almost always succeed in creating a species of practical discretion in democracies, and that science of the daily occurrences

---

[29] For figures on the growing cost of American foreign policy, see J. L. McCamy, *The Administration of American Foreign Affairs* (New York, Knopf, 1950), pp. 3–7.

of life which is called good sense. Good sense may suffice to direct the ordinary course of society; and amongst a people whose education has been provided for, the advantages of democratic liberty in the internal affairs of the country may more than compensate for the evils inherent in a democratic government. But such is not always the case in the mutual relations of foreign nations.

.   .   .   .   .   .

Foreign politics demand scarcely any of those qualities which a democracy possesses; and they require, on the contrary, the perfect use of almost all those faculties in which it is deficient. Democracy is favourable to the increase of the internal resources of the State; it tends to diffuse a moderate independence; it promotes the growth of public spirit, and fortifies the respect which is entertained for law in all classes of society; and these are advantages which only exercise an indirect influence over the relations which one people bears to another. But a democracy is unable to regulate the details of an important undertaking, to persevere in a design, and to work out its execution in the presence of serious obstacles. It cannot combine its measures with secrecy, and it will not await their consequences with patience. These are qualities which more especially belong to an individual or to an aristocracy; and they are precisely the means by which an individual people attains to a predominant position. . . .[30]

When Alexis de Tocqueville published these sentiments over a century ago, he admitted that they were in the nature of a hypothesis which was still incapable of proof. In his sense of the term, the United States was the unique democracy of

---

[30] Alexis de Tocqueville, *Democracy in America*, trans. Henry Reeve (London, Longmans, 1835), Vol. I, pp. 236–37.

his time; its history, once its independence had been fully established and maintained, had hitherto presented it with no important problems in the sphere of foreign policy; one would have to wait and see.

As we have already seen, an American historian, writing on what proved to be the eve of America's entry into the First World War, could suggest that prophecies such as those of Tocqueville had proved beside the mark. In presenting the world with a new edition of his book in 1923, he did not find it necessary to repudiate his earlier views. He had previously given it as his opinion that American success in foreign affairs had been closely connected with the American devotion to neutrality and to noninvolvement. "With such a task as keeping adjusted a balance of power, democracy is probably incompetent to deal; with its accustomed practicality the democracy of America had determined that it will have no balance of power in America and will not meddle with it where it exists."[31] Now with the war, these conditions had changed; but the American people had not swerved from their position. It had been natural for them to have recourse to a world organization whose legalistic procedures would be analogous to the way in which they were accustomed to handling affairs at home. The essential effect would be not entangling but disentangling.

In fact by this time, the American people—or at any rate its representatives—had chosen a simpler method of disentanglement. But these vicissitudes did not at the time seem to thoughtful Americans to cast any real doubt on the validity

---

[31] Fish, *American Diplomacy* (New York, Holt, 1923), p. 500.

of their fundamental political beliefs. In 1924, a distinguished member of the foreign service published a systematic study of the whole problem. His conclusion might serve as not unrepresentative of views held here at that time:

> The conduct of foreign relations under the rapidly developing conditions of modern democracy is a vital and fascinating problem. Those who have faith in the democratic principle must suffer discouragement at times, rather through eagerness and impatience on their own part. The popular sense of responsibility and restraint which is essential to peace in a democratic world will grow as foreign affairs come increasingly within the popular knowledge, and the wisdom of the popular judgment, when it is deliberately expressed, is a foundation upon which a lasting edifice may be built.[32]

Thirty years have elapsed since those words were written; it would be hard to maintain that they do not provide us with adequate material for yet another inquiry into the legitimacy of Tocqueville's thesis.

---

[32] DeWitt C. Poole, *The Conduct of Foreign Relations under Modern Democratic Conditions* (New Haven, Yale University Press, 1924), pp. 196–97.

II *The Presuppositions*
OF DEMOCRATIC FOREIGN POLICY

Iₙ SETTING THE PROBLEM OF DEMOCRATIC FOR-
eign policy—which is first and most obviously a problem of
the public mind—it is not desirable to make too early the
distinction that the scholar would naturally draw between
diplomacy and foreign policy. Indeed, even the scholar is not
always clear on this distinction, since we talk for instance of
diplomatic history when what clearly concerns us is as much
the content and fate of particular policies as the methods
adopted for their execution. Nevertheless there comes a point
at which some attempt to draw the line is at least helpful.

In his book *Modern Democracies*, Lord Bryce who combined in his own person the scholar and the man of affairs,
devoted a chapter to the subject of "Democracy and Foreign
Policy." Although the book was not published until 1921, this
chapter was written in 1918, at a time when the question had
been brought forcibly before public attention by the activities
and pronouncements of President Woodrow Wilson. The distinction that Bryce drew was one between "ends and means."
He did not accept the view that democracies were by their
nature incapable of generating an intelligent and realistic
view of where their interests lay or that they were incapable
of holding fast to a consistent line of policy. He believed that
the contrary could be demonstrated both by the record of the
United States and by that of the French Republic, despite
its notorious turnover in governments. In the case of his own
country, Britain, he argued that in most of the disputed
issues in foreign policy in recent times, and most notably in
the case of the American Civil War, the instinct of the broad
masses of the British people had proved more nearly right

than that of the majority of the governing class. On the other hand, he did not believe that in the execution of foreign policy, the role of executive government could easily be diminished or that Parliament could take a more direct role. "The Means," he wrote, "used for attaining the Ends sought cannot be safely determined by legislatures so long as our international relations continue to be what they have heretofore been, because secrecy is sometimes and expert knowledge is always required."[1]

This difference between "ends" and "means" commended itself more easily to an elder statesman like Bryce than to the broad masses in Europe who, reeling under the shock of the most devastating of wars, were in a mood to listen to any suggestion that by taking the conduct of foreign affairs into their own hands they could be spared a repetition of the holocaust. In the denunciations of the "secret treaties" between the Allies (whose publication by the Bolsheviks remains on record as their single most successful piece of propaganda) it was far from clear whether the indignation expressed sprang from the alleged iniquity of the contents of those agreements, or from the mere fact that they had been negotiated under conditions of secrecy, and had remained undivulged. Even to this day, one finds some uncertainty on this point.

A former British diplomat whose mordant diary of the Paris Peace Conference did much to shape later Anglo-Saxon opinion on that event, has since gone so far as to say that some attempt at a more popular diplomacy at that time was

---

[1] Lord Bryce, *Modern Democracies* (London, Macmillan, 1921), vol. 2, p. 420.

in fact inevitable. But, since the initiative was actually Wilson's, he believes that one could call the new method, the "American method." As he points out, Wilson himself was swift to realize once he got to Paris that he could not keep literally to his idea that "diplomacy should proceed always frankly and in the public view." Wilson took the view that only the publication of the conclusions reached was essential and that there was "nothing that need deter him from"—I quote the writer who was there—"conducting prolonged negotiations with Lloyd George and Clemenceau, while one American marine stood with fixed bayonet at the study door, and another patrolled the short strip of garden outside." But this shift was, in this writer's view, never grasped by public opinion, so that the identification of diplomacy with its results remains, he tells us, "perhaps the most confusing of all the fallacies that we owe to President Wilson."[2]

It is clear that the view that relations between countries could be conducted in the public forum was a principal source of public support for the two successive attempts at world organization—the League of Nations and the United Nations—that have been made in the aftermath of the two world wars. Indeed, in my own view, this aspect of their functioning has made a much greater popular appeal than the "collective security" or "super-state" idea which has carried conviction only where its possible consequences for one's own nation have not been fully appreciated.

During the flourishing period of the League's history, popu-

---

[2] Sir Harold Nicolson, *The Evolution of Diplomatic Method* (London, Constable, 1954), pp. 85–6.

lar expectations about the possibility of conducting foreign policy openly seemed to be at least partially fulfilled. While it could not be said that the League's members had abandoned the use of more conventional diplomatic methods, the speeches made at Geneva were of real significance in defining national attitudes; and for a time, as far at least as Europe was concerned, the Geneva tribune was the focal point of international relations. It ceased to be so only when the objectives of some powers became such that neither the fulfilment of their aims nor the concerting of resistance to them could be handled in this way to any significant degree.[3]

The United Nations Organization has not hitherto had even the League's temporary success. Owing to the fact that the principal participating powers were from the beginning of the Organization's existence deeply divided by hostility and mutual fear, there could be no genuine dialogue between them. And the forum which the United Nations provided was at once used not for public diplomacy but for two quite different purposes. On the one hand, it provided a platform from which representative statesmen could exhort their own nationals to greater efforts by branding the iniquities of their opponents; on the other hand, it gave them an opportunity for appealing not to the governments of unfriendly powers nor even to those governments still unaligned with either bloc

---

[3] This fact should not of course lead the historian of those years to overlook other and less praiseworthy activities of some of the Geneva heroes, as is done to some extent by F. P. Walters in his otherwise excellent *History of the League of Nations* (London, 1952), 2 vols.

but to the peoples behind those governments. It is indeed the reaction against the apparent exacerbation of international tensions by these purely propagandist activities that underlies the new affection for the "old diplomacy" shown by some British writers, and less ostentatiously by some Americans— an affection which in the post-Stalin period has acquired some seeming respectability even in Soviet circles.

The legitimacy of the use in diplomacy of an appeal over the heads of governments to the peoples is a question with an involved and curious but illuminating history. It is of course the natural recourse of revolutionary regimes, since if their message is universalist, they must assume that the masses of the people in other countries are really on their side, and are only prevented from proclaiming the fact by the oppression under which they are suffering. When the Bolsheviks from the very first days of their regime began the equivocal course which they have usually followed since then, of appealing simultaneously to foreign governments, and to foreign peoples, they were doing no more than revive a tactic familiar to Revolutionary France.

It is otherwise with the statesmen of the parliamentary democracies. If they are sufficiently convinced of the unchallengeable rightness of their own cause they may be tempted, as was President Wilson in 1919, to assume that those foreign leaders who oppose them are unrepresentative of their people, and that the latter will repudiate them if the facts of the situation can be made known. They are liable if they act on this assumption to get the kind of rebuke which the Italian Prime Minister addressed to Wilson: "to place the Italian people in opposition to the government would be to admit that this great free nation would submit to the yoke of a will other than its own, and I should be forced to protest strongly against suppositions unjustly offensive to my country."[4] But the temptation is always present when more normal diplomatic methods appear to be gaining no ground. It is not for a foreign observer to say whether the statements of the American Secretary of State or of the German Chancellor in the crisis over the European Defence Community in the late summer of 1954 were intended to rally opposition against the French Prime Minister in his own country. But the fact that these statements were so interpreted, and being so interpreted may have contributed to strengthening his position, as President Wilson strengthened Orlando's, shows that the question is by no means a closed one.

Even where there is no recourse to this particular form of open diplomacy, it is worth remembering that the necessity of justifying one's policies to the home parliament and electorate may inadvertently cause embarrassment to a friendly government. A classic blunder of this kind is attributable to no less a master of diplomatic art than the great Lord Salisbury. Commending an Anglo-French agreement on spheres of influence in Africa in a speech to the House of Lords, Salisbury was naturally concerned to show that its terms were favorable to Britain. "Anyone who looks at the map," he said in conclusion, "and merely measures degrees" would perhaps think that France had laid claim to a very considerable area "but it is necessary to judge land not merely from extent but

---

[4] Declaration of Signor Orlando, April 24, 1919, quoted by DeWitt C. Poole, *The Conduct of Foreign Relations*, pp. 32–33.

also from value. This land is what agriculturists would call very "light" land. It is the desert of Sahara. . . ." For the French Ambassador occupying his seat in the gallery and representing a government which had hoped to revive its prestige by the announcement of this very agreement, these lightly-spoken words took on a very different air, and he could not forbear protesting; "No doubt," he wrote to Lord Salisbury, "the Sahara is not a garden, and contains as you say much light land; but your public reminder of the fact was, perhaps you will allow me to say, hardly necessary. You might well have left us to find it out."[5]

More tempting and more common is the use or attempted use of this weapon against powers that are neither friendly nor democratic. Orlando, in his protest against Wilson's appeal to the Italians, referred to his "regret in recalling that this process, heretofore applied to enemy Governments, is today applied for the first time to a Government which has been and intends to remain a loyal ally of the great American Republic." Whether or not it be effective, its use against enemy governments in wartime, particularly if they are themselves nondemocratic, has become almost a matter of course. However fantastic it may seem in retrospect, in the light of what we now know to have been the cohesiveness of the German system under the Nazis, until the very eve of its collapse, Britain did in fact begin the war against Germany in 1939 by sending over aircraft carrying not bombs, but leaflets. And clearly there might be circumstances—such

---

[5] A. L. Kennedy, *Salisbury, 1830–1903* (London, Murray, 1953), p. 225.

as did not exist in this instance—where attempts to appeal to the population, or even the armed forces of a hostile power, might be justified.

The argument has been carried a stage further by those who feel that this method is suited to dealing with regimes with whom a nominal state of peace exists, but which are regarded as inherently inimical to the democracies concerned. We must assume that President Roosevelt's personal appeals to the dictators in April, 1939, were directed more to the peoples they controlled than to individuals whose lack of devotion to peace had by then been made abundantly clear. (No doubt the President had public opinion at home in mind also.) And although one would hesitate before appearing to equate Jefferson Davis with Hitler or Mussolini, President Lincoln's first inaugural address was based upon similar assumptions about the real temper of the South.

In more recent times the idea of appealing over the heads of the Soviet rulers, if not to the Russian people then at least to the peoples of the satellites, has figured largely in discussions of the kind of policy the Western powers might follow other than the purely defensive one to which they are committed, from the military point of view, by the evident abhorrence of all democracies for the idea of preventive war. Indeed a more vigorous attempt to communicate with the captive peoples of Europe appears to have been what was meant by the distinction between "containment" and "liberation" which the change of administration in Washington at the beginning of 1953 was expected to bring about. So at least one might judge from the strong advocacy of such efforts in the book *War or Peace,* which the new Secretary of State had published a couple of years earlier.[6]

Mr. John Foster Dulles was too experienced and too intelligent a statesman not to be aware of the dangers of such activities. In demanding that American policy should concentrate upon "activating" the latent difficulties of the Communist empire, he was emphatic in pointing out that "activation" did not mean "armed revolt." "The people," he wrote, "have no arms, and violent revolt would be futile. Indeed it would be worse than futile, for it would precipitate massacre."[7] And his subsequent conduct in office followed this line, even to the extent of making some people feel that the new liberation was only the old containment "writ large."

It does not follow, however, that the average citizen of a democracy is as ready as was Mr. Dulles to appreciate the very vital difference between psychological warfare as an adjunct to armed combat, and its very limited usefulness when armed force is ruled out. "Some men," we read in a recent study of American policy, "have unwisely recommended the policy of pinpricks, the stirrings of revolt which would be foredoomed to bloody repression—a course which, however much it might satisfy our feelings of hatred for the Communist tyranny, would be impractical and cruel."[8] Indeed one could go further and say that many men will be tempted to

---

[6] John Foster Dulles, *War or Peace* (New York, Macmillan, 1950), p. 247.

[7] *Ibid.* p. 247.

[8] Thomas K. Finletter, *Power and Policy* (New York, Harcourt-Brace, 1954), p. 123.

recommend policies of this type because this kind of democratic diplomacy corresponds so closely to one of the fundamental preconceptions or presuppositions which make democracies adopt the kind of foreign policies which they tend to prefer. In other words, a discussion of technique leads one inevitably into the much broader questions of policy and of general attitudes towards foreign affairs.

Before following this lead, it is important to realize how pervasive is this belief that the existence of public opinion in foreign countries is a utilizable political asset. The appeal to it need not be as direct as on some of the occasions already mentioned. Indeed, it finds its most familiar embodiment in what has come to be the characteristically American use of the doctrine of nonrecognition. The traditional view about the right of a foreign government to be recognized, like most other matters of international law, has been the product of usage. By and large it resolves itself into the simple formula that, since one cannot avoid dealing with foreign governments if they control any area in which one's own country has an interest, the only test of whether or not they should be recognized is a factual one. Is the government in question really in control of the national territory, or the most important part of it, and is it likely to remain so? Clearly this question only arises normally as a result of revolution or of foreign conquest. There may always be a pause; but sooner or later the issue has got to be faced; either the revolutionary regime (or the one imposed by military force) has maintained itself, or it has failed to do so, in which case the question is at once renewed over its successor.

Democracies—and the American democracy in particular

—have never been very happy over this version of the problem. By an analogy from private life in which one chooses one's friends, they tend to assume that it is possible to choose the governments with whom one has dealings and to ignore those of whose ideologies or practices one disapproves. Normally however this assertion of the right to choose nonrecognition is coupled with the belief, avowed or unavowed, that nonrecognition will itself solve the problem by leading to the overthrow of the regime towards which the antipathy is felt. Although circumstances can be imagined in which this would be the case (nonrecognition by France would hardly be long survived by the government of the Principality of Monaco), history suggests that as with other forms of appealing to peoples against their rulers, the democratic liking for this weapon is ill advised.

Even relatively minor powers show considerable abilities to resist pressure of this kind. Such pressure may, if combined with active or covert support of a rival contender for power, achieve the object of forcing out the actual government in question. Wilson did in fact get rid of Huerta in Mexico; but the expectation that a positive influence for good could thereby be exercised was not realized. If Wilson's purpose was as he said to "teach the South American republics to elect good men," he was not immediately successful.[9] Where as in the case of the rather watered-down attempt to eliminate the Franco regime in Spain by a kind of general diplomatic boycott after the Second World War, there is no

---

[9] Arthur S. Link, *Woodrow Wilson and the Progressive Era, 1910–1917* (New York, Harper and Bros., 1954), Chap. 5.

alternative regime to which general support can be given, the policy is even less likely to yield results.

But the appeal to democracies of tactics which could seemingly achieve so much at such little cost is so great that, in the American public mind at any rate, this has become a method for dealing not only with small powers but even with great ones. For the original refusal of most Western countries to have dealings with the Soviet regime, perfectly good arguments were available. For some time after the Bolshevik Revolution, rival regimes were in being, commanding sizable military forces and, at times, important areas of the national territory. Since under conditions of civil war and of terror on both sides, the application to Russia of the principle of self-determination was not obvious, the Allied governments could reasonably hold their hands in the hope that the Bolsheviks' enemies (to whom they were giving some, though inadequate, aid) would triumph and thus remove the dilemma. Once the Bolsheviks had won the civil war and thrown back the Polish invasion, this argument ceased to have validity; and after some hesitation, most European countries accepted the applicability of the traditional argument and accorded recognition. The Americans with fewer direct interests involved could afford to follow the democratic impulse and deny recognition as a sign of their disapproval—a disapproval shared by most Europeans—of the policies of the Soviet Union both at home and abroad.

By the time that the United States had decided that no useful purpose was being served by this demonstration, it was engaged in using the same tactic with regard to changes brought about not by revolution but by conquest. It could be argued that the Stimson doctrine of nonrecognition, promulgated with regard to the Japanese puppet-state of Manchukuo, was better founded than the idea of non-recognition based upon an abhorrence of revolution. For the Chinese government still existed and still claimed what it regarded as China's eastern provinces; and, while that was so, it was plausible to hold that the Japanese conquest was a temporary one toward which every expression of disapproval was legitimate. On the other hand, as it appeared in the public mind, nonrecognition of the Stimson variety went further than this; it was itself a method of denying to Japan, without any sacrifice on one's own part, the full fruits of her aggression. And in the sense that while it persisted Japan would regard the United States as a hostile if nonbelligerent power, it was indeed much more than an empty gesture. No subject is likely to intrigue the diplomatic historian longer than that of American-Japanese relations in the decade after 1931; but however the story may come to be told in detail, it is unlikely that anyone will seriously deny that the ultimate roots of the Pacific war are to be found in the denial by the United States of Japan's right to seek a forcible solution to her problems on the Asiatic mainland. Attempts made to seek a compromise on some of the practical issues involved landed the American government in serious difficulties with important sections of opinion at home.[10] In other words, the doctrine of nonrecognition led on this occasion to its logical conclusion—intervention by force against the offending regime—a policy which if

---

[10] See, for example, F. C. Jones, *Japan's New Order* (London, 1954), p. 310.

directly presented to a democratic electorate will rarely, if ever, be found to have a popular appeal.

The issue of nonrecognition in regard to a revolutionary regime came up once more in the case of Communist China. And once again a division made itself apparent between the American view, on the one hand, and that of Great Britain, on the other. As in the Russian case, as in every case, the elements of the situation were not identical for the powers concerned. These differences have had sufficient airing; on the British side, the influence of the Asiatic members of the Commonwealth, economic interests, the lesser impact of the Korean war, or if one prefers it, the greater surviving impact of the Nazi war in Europe; on the American side, the emotional commitment involved in the wartime belief—so strenuously and vainly challenged by Sir Winston Churchill who called it "the great American illusion"[11]—that postwar China would be a strong and reliable bulwark of peace in the East, and later the strategic importance attached to Formosa and its guardian Seventh Fleet, above all, once more, the deep conviction that Communism is an internal as well as an external foe—a conviction now working in favour of more rigid policies abroad. Nevertheless, the actual arguments, however important in their impact on the public mind, in either country, should not be allowed to conceal the fact that the question of recognizing Communist China was not fundamentally different from other historical examples of the same kind of dilemma.

---

[11] Herbert Feis, *The China Tangle* (Princeton University Press, 1953), p. 284.

Either, the Chinese Communist government should have been regarded as established in its authority and likely to remain so in that kind of future perspective in which statesmen can properly deal, in which case recognition would be argued for on the conventional grounds; or else it should have been regarded as a transitory regime which its rival on Formosa might yet replace, in which case nonrecognition, as in the case of the Allies' early attitude to Soviet Russia, would be a clear declaration of hostility and ought, in logic, to lead to more active intervention to secure its overthrow. The difficulty would not seem to be one of logically defending either position, but rather of persuading democratic peoples that this kind of dilemma is likely to be inescapable in a world where many things are outside their control.

It will probably be realized that, by this approach to the question of democratic habits in international relations, one is likely to exclude what has been a favorite way of explaining their idiosyncrasies, especially by those who disapprove of them. Our British ex-diplomat, for instance, believes that what he calls the "new" or American method of diplomacy arose from "the belief that it was possible to apply to the conduct of *external* affairs, the ideas and practices which in the conduct of *internal* affairs, had for generations been regarded as the essentials of liberal democracy."[12] This view, while obviously not wholly without foundation, is surely a rather superficial one. Indeed, a former member of the State Department takes an almost precisely opposite view. What

---

[12] Sir Harold Nicolson, *The Evolution of Diplomatic Method,* p. 84.

intrigues him is that Americans who are so sceptical about government's efficiency for its internal task should be so ready to credit it with omnipotence abroad.[13] It is of course true that, in dealing with the unfamiliar, men think largely in terms of analogy; we have already seen how the recognition of an uncongenial government may be likened most misleadingly to shaking hands with a scoundrel. An American authority has noted—and correctly so—the proneness of democracies to seek moral justification for what can be justified at a lower level, and hence to turn all wars into crusades with highly deleterious effects upon the ultimate peacemaking. No doubt people do feel in some obscure way that assemblies like those of the League or of the United Nations and tribunals like the Permanent Court of International Justice do correspond, or should correspond, to the parliaments and law courts with which they are familiar at home.

But if people seriously believe that the substance of international life can be dealt with in this way, then it is not that the analogy is false, but that they have misconceived the essentials of liberal democracy in its domestic aspects. No doubt there is a sense in which legislatures enact laws, and courts dispense justice; but no one would think of describing the essential working of a society in terms of its parliamentary debates, or of pronouncements from the bench. These are, after all, merely the forms that we have chosen in modern times for the registry of decisions; the stuff of which they are composed is the result of a constantly shifting climate

---

[13] C. B. Marshall, *The Limits of American Foreign Policy* (New York, Henry Holt, 1954).

of opinion, and of the constant interaction of social groups seeking to bring about their separate aims by a judicious blending of pressures and of moral suasion. If the status, let us say, of trade-unions is not the same today in either Britain or America as it was a hundred, or even fifty, or even twenty years ago, this is the work neither of their legislators nor of their courts. Nor do I believe that the ordinary citizen has had to wait for the political scientist to expose some of the formal myths of the democratic process.

Confusion about institutions, and about their role, obviously exists and deserves exploration. But what the democratic citizen brings into the international field is a view not about institutions, or about methods, but about expectations. And again, a closer view of democratic politics on the internal side would help to suggest where the confusion is likely to arise. To take one point that has already been dealt with in another context: the direct appeal to foreign peoples. The social groupings within a modern democratic community do normally possess a certain fluidity. Of course loyalties exist, and in the case of some social groupings they may be so fierce that the penalties for ignoring them are severe. But their rigidities are not the same as the rigidities inherent in the national group. It is perfectly plausible to appeal for support on an internal issue to some new combination of groups, or behind a group's nominal leaders to the rank and file. Our whole electoral process would otherwise be meaningless. There is thus nothing unnatural in expecting similar tactics to profit one in dealing with foreign nations; it is a transfer of attitudes not of methods.

More fundamental is the nature of the content of democratic politics which is so largely concerned today with the disposition of scarce resources. The point here is that, for the most part, the political process tends to obfuscate this fact. Politicians, if they are to win elections, have normally got to argue that unpleasant choices need not be made, that higher farm prices need not mean paying more for food, that a rise in railroad wages need not be reflected in the cost of transport, and so on. These are recognized political gambits, and in a buoyant economy no one perhaps is much the worse. But in the relations between states into which the element of military power ineluctably intrudes, similar margins for error do not exist. By and large you can have the policy you are willing to pay for; no more, no less. It is no answer as some people think to say that this ignores the moral factor; for the moral factor is itself an element in a nation's power. If a state liquidates its military leadership as the Soviet Union did during the great purges, its value as an ally drops and its diplomatic position is correspondingly weakened. If a democratic country shows itself hopelessly divided internally, if doubts are cast on the loyalty and the intelligence of its public servants, if danger promotes a hunt for scapegoats rather than a search for remedies, that country's ability to exercise influence abroad is in fact diminished. There has been an actual loss of power.

But since democracies have not got the habit of strict accountancy at home, it is natural that they should avoid it in their foreign dealings, where the general unfamiliarity with the issues at stake makes the task anyhow more difficult. It may be that nations with a long experience of the complexities and dangers of life on the international scene acquire a certain readiness to allow for this by giving to their political leaders a freer hand abroad than they would at home; though, in view of the interpenetration of foreign policy and the domestic effort, this is not likely to be adequate in itself. And as the example of French policy in the nineteen-thirties may serve to remind us, even an historic nation may be too sharply divided for its instinct of self-preservation to function effectively. It may simply be that the older nations of Europe have retained, incapsulated within them, sufficient relics of their predemocratic leadership to provide the necessary ballast for the democratic sails. At any rate, whatever may be the case of older nations, newly enfranchised democracies would all seem to require at least a period of apprenticeship during which to learn the first lesson of foreign policy—the inescapable relation between policy and power, and the necessity of understanding that to make decisions affecting power independently of decisions affecting policy is the most gross of political errors. It would further seem to be true that some elements in a newly enfranchised democracy will learn this lesson earlier than others. It would finally seem to be the case—and some Americans have argued that it applies to their own history—that the lesson can be learned and then forgotten again.[14]

Students of American foreign policy have indeed dwelt much on the assumption of invulnerability which for almost a century conditioned public responses to events abroad and which was slow to change in the altered circumstances of later

[14] Walter Lippmann, *U. S. Foreign Policy, Shield of the Republic* (Boston, Little Brown, 1943).

years. Now in their turn, the American policy-makers and the American public often show irritation at such governments as that of India which appear to them to have been blind to the menace of Communist expansion. But there seems, as I have said, no reason to doubt the existence, as a general rule, of a close relation between a period of protection by an outside power and a subsequent reluctance to meet the demands made by the acquisition of independent responsibility for defense and an independent role in the formulation of foreign policy.

A remarkable example of this is provided by the development of Australian opinion on world affairs after the First World War. In that war the new nation's achievements had fortified the new status of total autonomy which it had gained. Since Australia had vast tasks to perform at home and no clear consciousness of any profound involvement with the external world, the immediate effect of these developments was to turn the nation in on itself. "Labour," writes an Australian historian, "the political party which was strongest on autonomy, made autonomy mean in practice a right to avoid international affairs."[15]

Nor indeed was it at first sight evident that such external involvement existed. Australia was only to a very slight degree a colonial power; she had no overseas ambitions and could feel that a limited contribution to British naval strength was sufficient to assure protection of her vital trade routes. The foundation of her national policy, the building up of a

---

[15] Paul Hasluck, *The Government and the People* (Canberra, 1952), pp. 5 ff.

high standard of living on the basis of protectionism and of highly selective immigration, insofar as it was not simply taken for granted by all Australians, seems to have been regarded as an aspect of domestic and not of foreign policy. That the "White Australia" policy might be domestic for her purposes, but provide a challenge to a crowded Orient, and in particular to Japan, and so in fact form the unacknowledged major premise of her foreign policy—this was a notion difficult, perhaps impossible, for the Australian people to entertain.

Granted this view of the peaceful and inoffensive nature of her own outlook, and the general belief that the League experiment had inaugurated a new era in world affairs, Australia's frame of mind is not hard to understand. The same Australian historian goes on to say:

> Perhaps Australia had entered the family of nations too easily, sponsored by a great power, and had never had occasion to meditate on the precarious existence of a small nation in a world of power. She had entered international life as a member of a League which, in the act of its foundation, had increased the number of small states and whose Covenant exalted the principles of self-determination and equal sovereignty, and she had never known anything of international affairs less kindly than the fussing of a motherland and the arguments of Geneva.

In Australia, there existed as a break upon illusion a body of political opinion convinced of the surviving value of the Imperial connection and determined that the way forward for Australia was through exerting greater influence in the affairs of the Empire as a whole.

Since in the inter-war years this section of opinion normally provided the federal governmental majority its effect upon policy and action was of course decisive. But it would be true to say that in a sense the attitude of labor was the more illuminating; nor in a country where labor was industrially as well as politically so influential could its attitude be without important consequences. Labor opinion in Australia, like radical opinion in Europe and America, tended in reaction against the First World War to seek for its origins in capitalism and imperialism. The Party's official leadership was not strictly pacifist, but it believed that Australian defenses could be secured by local action and that to participate in the plans of imperial strategists was to court the wars that all Australians sought to avoid. The avoidance of secret diplomacy, the control of foreign policy by the legislature, direct consultation of the people on important issues—these familiar slogans of the nineteen-thirties in the United States were actively propagated by the Australian labor leaders in the nineteen-twenties. These sentiments were generous in their origins; but the great depression tended to emphasize the division between classes in Australia and to impair the sense of national community and consequently of the national interest. Underlying differences over foreign policy were fundamental differences in social and political philosophy. Mere argument could hardly override them; only the impact of mortal danger could reduce them to due proportion and reassert the claims of national integrity.

Meanwhile Australian experiences provided an example of yet another phenomenon to which Americans will not find it hard to invoke parallels: the effect of preconceptions about foreign policy on the preference as between the weapons of war. Cruisers, the emblem of British naval strength, were naturally anathema to the labor protagonists of Australian autonomy who regarded them as by nature offensive. They only departed from their opposition to their acquisition to the extent of saying that, if there were to be any, they should be built in Australia so as to provide employment and keep the money in the country. In the phrase of a later day, there was to be no "offshore procurement." Instead of cruisers, defensive weapons were to be favored, and since neither a standing army nor compulsory training were acceptable to the labor mind, submarines and, above all, aircraft for coastal defense were advanced as the solution to the problem of Australia's security. Land-based aircraft and submarines —weapons which many other countries regarded as quintessentially offensive—became the symbol of Australian labor's determination to defend its homeland, and nothing beyond it.

The rise of European fascism and the more menacing (from the Australian viewpoint) inauguration of a new period of Japanese expansionism presented the Australian Labour party with a challenge parallel to the one facing similar political elements in other countries. Some leaders of the Australian Labour party, echoing in part the current Soviet interpretation of the world scene, denounced with considerable fervor the policies of "appeasement" followed by Britain and France. Indeed, a careful study of their pronouncements is needed in order to avoid falling into the error that what they advocated was a more extensive Australian commitment to the common defense.

Since the British Labour politicians of the period saw

nothing incongruous in demanding a firm front against the aggressor while opposing rearmament, there is no reason why their overseas brethren should have been more sophisticated. Some Australian Labour leaders cherished the belief that so-called working-class "sanctions," the direct refusal by Australian labor to load Japanese ships, would provide a way of hampering the aggressor without either risking war or conniving at capitalist foreign policies. The official leadership of the party held aloof, sadly admitting that collective security, while admirable as an ideal, was not suited to a nonsocialist world. As on the left in Britain, the war when it came modified many views. It was an expensive lesson.

This problem of false expectations—and there are many other examples—seems to me much more significant for our subject than the often used argument that democracies cannot handle foreign affairs because they are ignorant of them. It was this aspect of them that struck an American diplomat writing thirty years ago. He thought that the dangers which democracies feared because of information that was allegedly kept back from them were largely illusory. "I venture the thought," he wrote," "that the problem of the modern foreign minister, seeking legislative and popular support, is often how to get people to absorb more information rather than to keep information from them."[16] The United States government would seem to have accepted this viewpoint. The foreign observer is struck by the sustained effort of the State Department, through publications and through lectures by its senior officers, to create an informed opinion; such activities fall

---

[16] DeWitt C. Poole, *The Conduct of Foreign Relations*, p. 156.

almost entirely outside the scope of the Foreign Office or the Quai d'Orsay. In this age when the study of public opinion is something between a morbid pre-occupation and big business, we can measure fairly closely the actual degree of public ignorance which remains.

A widely-publicized analysis of the United States scene from this point of view led in 1949 to the conclusion that; "about 30 per cent of the electorate, on the average, is *unaware* of almost any given event in American foreign affairs" and that "about 45 per cent of the electorate is *aware* of important events in the field but cannot be considered *informed*" and finally, that "only 25 per cent of the electorate consistently shows knowledge of foreign problems." And these blank figures are in turn susceptible to closer analysis; rural inhabitants being more ignorant than urban-dwellers, women than men, and so on.[17]

Even a people which should find it easier to grasp the possible effects of action in the field of foreign policy upon daily life may be no less hazy as to the content of particular proposals. A poll taken in France in the late spring of 1953 on the apparently crucial question of the European Defence Community produced the following:

"Four-fifths of the public," it was reported, "have heard about the project but are uncertain as to whether the plan had been passed or not. It is generally known that Germany would participate in the European Army but less generally

---

[17] Martin Kriesberg, "Dark Areas of Ignorance," *Public Opinion and Foreign Policy*, ed. Lester Markel (New York, Harper and Bros., 1949), p. 51.

that Britain would not participate. The idea of Europe receives the support of 70 per cent of the persons questioned; the idea of a European Army is accepted by rather less than half of the public with the opposition of around a quarter of it. The participation of Germany in the European Army is only accepted as a lesser evil. The project of the European Army as it was put forward at the time of the poll was embarrassing because it was little known."[18]

No doubt a similar revelation of public ignorance could be obtained by investigations in other democracies, not excluding Britain. The question is: what conclusions should be drawn from statistics of this kind? The American student whom I have been following has no doubt; "What happens in any quarter of the world has an effect on the life of even the humblest citizen, and he must be made to realize it." He assumes that the situation not only should but can be changed; the only problem is that of the method. "What is to be done?" he asks. "How can apathy and indifference be transformed into an active interest in foreign affairs? How can ignorant and prejudiced people be transformed into a well-informed tolerant electorate?"[19]

Discussion in these terms seems to be based once more, at least in part, upon an unreal estimate of how a democratic system works even in internal affairs. It is of course desirable that there should be throughout the community, and particu-

---

[18] Pierre Gerbert, "L'influence de l'opinion publique et des partis sur la politique étrangère en France," *La Politique Etrangère et ses Fondements* (Paris, Presses Universitaires, 1954), p. 87.

[19] Martin Kriesberg, "Dark Areas of Ignorance," *op. cit.*, p. 63.

larly in positions of influence persons well-informed about the issues of foreign policy that confront the nation's government. Again the work of voluntary bodies in this field throughout the country is, for a foreigner, an impressive aspect of the American scene. But most questions even of internal policy are too complicated and too technical for one to demand more of the ordinary citizen than some sense of the general trend of his social preferences, and some ability to relate to them the claims of rival parties where these exist. In the case of foreign affairs, where the given elements in a situation consist largely of the attitudes and intentions of foreign communities, to expect a very high level of information on the part of the electorate is surely utopian. Perhaps the clue to the confusion of thought is contained in the use of the words "well-informed and tolerant" in the passage quoted.

These qualities while both desirable are by no means identical. What one means by "tolerant" in such a context is surely no more than a readiness to accept the limitations on the ordinary citizen's knowledge and some capacity for critically accepting the leadership offered by those in a position to be better informed. The citizen must be prepared to accept a modification, where changing circumstances demand it, not only of inherited prejudices but even of those general presuppositions about foreign policy which are, as we have seen, so important a source of error.

A French commentator on the figures we have quoted makes a more realistic point in calling attention to the difference between the active and presumably more or less informed political minority and the mass of public opinion. If the former element proposes a line of policy the presumption will be in its favor, unless it runs counter to a very strong current of public opinion which is firmly wedded to some general principle which it feels is being set aside.[20] Experience in other democratic countries would appear to bear this out.

For this reason, it is important to grasp that, important as may be the presuppositions of a particular democracy, and the effect upon them of greater or lesser areas of ignorance concerning this or that aspect of foreign affairs, these things only take on meaning when considered in relation to action. This means that as far as modern democratic societies are concerned they become of concrete significance only within a particular institutional framework. The problem of democratic foreign policy has been largely a problem of the adequacy of democratic institutions. And here, although the problem is one of general significance, the actual situation differs so much from country to country and is often so unclear even in the minds of the citizens of each that quite particular caution is required in handling it.

A discussion of this subject also tends to generate heat because it may involve a challenge to the status of some institution with which one party to the dispute identifies its own weight and prestige. Senators cannot be impartial about the role of the Senate. Furthermore it itself involves certain rather widespread prejudices, notably the democratic suspicion of claims to expertise in politics. A writer whose claim for "democratized foreign affairs" we have already noted puts the point with some force: "professional pride, profes-

---

[20] Pierre Gerbert, "L'influence de l'opinion," *op. cit.*, p. 91.

sional defensiveness, tends in every field to discount the layman. It tends to build up a cult of expertness, an almost mystical cloud-throne guarded by the cherubim of a special technical language." He does not consider that Parliamentary questioning or Congressional hearings provide an adequate popular control over the expert: "not until there is broader participation in the planning, the development, and the execution of foreign policy can it be said that the people take part in their own foreign relations."[21]

When one comes to look into it and takes the writer's own examples of popular participation—the unofficial consultants used by the American delegation at the San Francisco Conference in 1945, or the work of the United States commission for UNESCO, of which he was himself a member—it becomes clear that by the layman, he does not mean the ordinary uninformed citizen who could clearly contribute very little at this level, but simply another kind of expert—the expert who is not in government service.

Thus the use of a familiar vocabulary of prejudice may conceal the fact that what is being discussed is again a perfectly legitimate and perennial question about institutions— the point at which the expert—civilian or soldier, government employee or private consultant—can most usefully be fitted in to the general scheme of policy-making and policy-execution. The best way of handling this topic is to consider not the institutions themselves one by one but rather the functions which they have to fulfill.

---

[21] James Marshall, "Citizen Diplomacy," *American Political Science Review* (February, 1944), p. 84.

III

The Institutions
OF DEMOCRATIC FOREIGN POLICY

THE CONDUCT OF FOREIGN POLICY INVOLVES A series of decisions and operations of which actual negotiation forms only a relatively small part. All the aspects of the decision-making process are interconnected, and to consider them separately is only justified insofar as it can contribute to clarity of thought. The principal share of attention in as far as the United States is concerned has recently been focussed on the objectives of foreign policy.[1] What are the interests that policy is concerned with protecting or promoting? From the point of view of the handling of such problems the dispute over moral purposes as contrasted with concrete material interests is largely beside the point. There are no doubt national differences of emphasis; I find it easy to accept what two American political scientists have recently argued that "the glory and aggrandizement of the nation-state are not for Americans synonymous with national interest," and understand their hope that "America's root concern, its ultimate concept of the national interest, may be the spreading and sharing, with due adaptation and without intolerance of its societal blessings."[2] But I would suggest that the attempt that they, and others have made, to draw a rather sharp line between this and European attitudes may be misdirected. It would seem to be the case that all nations

---

[1] See, for example, Dexter Perkins, *The American Approach to Foreign Policy* (Cambridge, Harvard University Press, 1952).

[2] Thomas I. Cook and Malcolm C. Moos, "The American Idea of National Interest," *American Political Science Review* (January, 1953), p. 33. Cf. John J. McCloy, *The Challenge to American Foreign Policy* (Cambridge, Harvard University Press, 1953), p. 25.

allow their policy to be influenced by their predilections for one kind of social order as against another, and that the extent to which they allow this to affect action will depend on the way in which their governmental institutions regard their own power, whether or not they see it as being capable of affecting events in the outside world. How they regard their power will again depend upon the extent to which they are subject to popular pressures—since the margin available to the state for the exercise of its moral predilections will tend to seem greater to the electorate than to the government, and greater perhaps to the civilian side of government than to the military. If Canning or Palmerston were able to give freer reign to their ideological preferences than their twentieth-century successors, it is not—as some people seem to think—that Britons have become less moral, but that Britain's relative power in the world has declined with the growth of the continental super-powers, and the increasing domination of the air weapon.

The institutional problem of relating foreign policy to budgetary policy in its widest aspects is perhaps the crucial point at which the shape of a country's institutional framework begins to count for most, both in its formal aspects and in its no less important informal ones—the party system for instance. There may have been a tendency to oversimplify this in terms of the controversies over foreign aid programs; but this, while natural enough because overseas expenditure makes no *prima facie* appeal to the taxpayer or his representatives, is unfortunate. The same problem would exist even if United States policy were to be based on the principle of hemispheric defense. The expenditure on such defense and to some extent the form that such expenditure took would still be dictated by a certain though different concept of foreign policy and by the calculations arising from it.

Although the problem of the relationship between military and foreign policy was fairly thoroughly canvassed in restricted circles in the United States from the eighteen-nineties at least, its significance did not achieve widespread recognition until the Second World War. Even then the problem which it posed for the structure of government was largely masked by the singularly personal and informal nature of President Roosevelt's leadership in this as in other fields. Some attempt had been made to create an institutional framework for handling the whole complex of questions even before the end of the war by means of interdepartmental committees; and the need to press on with this effort was given greater urgency when the President's guiding hand was so suddenly removed. Unlike his predecessor, President Truman preferred to work through his official advisers and to see business more tidily conducted; the episode leading to Henry Wallace's departure from his Cabinet suggests that the President's objective was not immediately achieved.

From the National Security Act of 1947 and down to the present, much of the history of United States government has been concerned with bringing defense, foreign and economic policies into proper focus.[3] An impetus to the process was given by important shifts in policy itself, such as that which

---

[3] On the early history of the National Security Council see Sidney W. Souers, "Policy Formulation for National Security," *American Political Science Review* (June, 1949), pp. 534 ff. Its

turned the original Marshall Plan program with its heavily economic and social emphasis into a primarily military mutual security program.[4] If one is to accept rather formidable recent criticisms of the current arrangements for settling the defense program—in which a purely budgetary approach seems to have got the upper hand—the period of experiment should not yet be over. "Power and policy" have proved difficult to align. On the other hand, some people fear that the solution most often advocated—the enhancement of the powers of the civilian heads of the service departments, and in particular of the Secretary of Defense—would give purely military considerations too great a weight in the shaping of policy, since such civilian heads would always be the prisoners of the men in uniform.

"For some reason," writes an American authority on these problems, "people are always expecting the American cabinet to be more signficant than it has been in recent years. Perhaps its name suggests the power of the British cabinet; perhaps British visitors who lecture in the United States about their superior ways have made us feel inferior."[5] I shall conform to precedent so far as to suggest that it is not altogether surprising that American reformers should have been attracted by the British system, with its initial advantage in

---

operation has since undergone important changes. President Eisenhower, unlike his predecessor, has for instance, normally attended its meetings in person.

[4] See Arthur W. Macmahon, *Administration in Foreign Affairs* (University of Alabama Press, 1953).

[5] J. L. McCamy, *The Administration of American Foreign Affairs*, p. 142.

the existence of a single decision-making body, and in the latter's capacity for effectual delegation either to the old Imperial Defence Committee or to the modern Defence Committee of the Cabinet.[6] In a note from General Wedemeyer to General Marshall in 1943, the former referred to "that unity of national effort which is so well exemplified in the British defence organisation."[7] But one should of course avoid exaggeration.

In the pre-1914 period crucial decisions of foreign policy were taken without full cabinet consultation and in the circumstances the military got considerable elbow room. Thus during the Agadir crisis the War Office itself actually settled technical details of military co-operation with the French; though on whose authorization it is even now not possible to say.[8] About later periods in the formation of British policy we know even less. The actual workings of the British system during the Second World War have received, so far, much less public documentation than their American counterparts; and the radiance shed by Sir Winston Churchill's memoirs may (like other searchlights) have had the effect of making the untouched part of the landscape blacker than ever. Certainly, the functioning of the system before and since the war is something about which dogmatism would be most unwise. For

---

[6] See H. D. Jordan, "The British Cabinet and the Ministry of Defence," *American Political Science Review* (February, 1949).

[7] Ray S. Cline, *Washington Command Post: The Operations Division*, ser. *The United States Army in World War II* (Washington, 1951), pp. 317–18.

[8] A. J. P. Taylor, *The Struggle for Mastery in Europe, 1848–1918*, p. 470.

all the ink that has been spilled over the conduct of British foreign policy under the premiership of Mr. Neville Chamberlain, we do not yet know in what form the underlying military problems of the period came up for consideration. What we do know is that Mr. Chamberlain's methods of conducting foreign policy were almost as personal and untidy as those of President Roosevelt, and that if the Foreign Office never became the cipher that the State Department seemingly was during the latter part of Mr. Cordell Hull's tenure and the incumbency of Mr. Stettinius, its role was hardly that allotted to it in the conventional textbooks of British government. And of course, even if the British system were the best that could be devised for solving this or any other problem, it could not in fact be grafted onto the presidential system without changing the whole nature of American government and politics to an unthinkable degree. In the last resort, what matters is who has the president's ear, and who the president is. Of all forms of democratic government the American depends most on the accident of personality.

As is well known, it is not the internal arrangements of the executive branch of the American government that most perplex the foreigner. He is likely to attach more importance to the independent role of Congress in providing the wherewithal for defense and foreign policies. The position of Congress appears to Englishmen especially, as an obstacle to that joint planning for the future on the part of the British and American government to which so many of them attach importance. "From our point of view," writes a former British Chancellor of the Exchequer, "we should welcome a greater unity in the thought about United States foreign policy and in the presentation of it, and my impression is that until this is achieved, both as between the Administration and the legislature and as between the parties, the working out of a common policy between Britain and America will continue to be gravely handicapped."[9] To some extent, the critics are only repeating what foreign statesmen said about nineteenth-century Britain's inability to maintain continuity of policy. Lord Salisbury wrote of the 1887 Mediterranean agreement: "it is as close an alliance as the Parliamentary character of our institution will permit."[10] One could add that the appearance of incoherence may not only discourage friends, but also mislead and encourage foes—and with possibly disastrous results.

The greater importance of the budgetary element has of necessity increased the share of Congress in the sphere of foreign policy, and more particularly that of the House of Representatives. The new position has been put with authority and clarity by an eminent member of that body: "As United States leadership has grown, so has the necessity for legislative formulation and implementation of foreign policy correspondingly increased. In practice the Congress has become an equal partner with the Executive in giving substance to United States leadership. In many instances the Congress on its own initiative has supplied direction to American foreign policy by establishing principles which are now guiding the United States in its relationship to the rest of the world."[11]

---

[9] Hugh Gaitskell, "The Search for an Anglo-American Policy," *Foreign Affairs* (July, 1954), p. 576.

[10] A. J. P. Taylor, *op. cit.*, p. 311.

[11] Chester E. Murrow, "Congress and Foreign Relations," *Annals* (September, 1953), p. 8.

And an acknowledged authority on Congress has written in the same vein: "more and more in fact as under the Constitution, Congress is a co-ordinate member of a foreign policy team; and this co-ordinate membership extends to the House as well as the Senate."[12]

The European student cannot but be impressed with the truth of such judgments, particularly in the light of recent history. It is clear, for instance, that it was from Congressional circles that the original initiative came for using American economic aid to bring about not merely economic co-operation between the countries of Europe but also their political integration in some federal form. The administration was at the beginning very doubtful about this approach, and opposed such proposals on the ground that they would look like interference with the domestic affairs of the European states, and so provide material for Communist propaganda. With the appropriations under the Mutual Security Act of 1951 being directed to "further encourage the economic unification and the political federation of Europe," and with Congress indicating in the act of 1952 that it believed it essential that the act "should be so administered as to support concrete measures for political federation, military integration and economic unification in Europe,"[13] the way

---

[12] E. S. Griffith, "Congress and Foreign Relations," *Annals* (September, 1953), p. 11.

[13] R. Dennett and K. D. Durant, eds., *Documents on American Foreign Relations, 1951* (Boston, World Peace Foundation, 1952), p. 128; C. W. Baier and R. P. Stebbins, eds., *Documents on American Foreign Relations, 1952* (New York, Harper and Bros., 1953), p. 39.

was clear for the appropriation under the act of 1953 to make assistance in part conditional upon ratification of the European Defence Community. The legislative history of the mutual security programs does not account for everything. Indeed a study of the origins and development of the EDC idea would probably provide an excellent example of how policies may gain a momentum of their own which carries them beyond their original objectives. It is a story which is still by no means fully elucidated. Various developments in the world scene had preceded the original American decision to ask its partners in the North Atlantic Pact to agree to a measure of German rearmament. There were the events in Czechoslovakia and other manifestations of increasing East-West tension in Europe which led to the North Atlantic Pact itself—a treaty which also owed something of its final shape to the pressure exercised by Congress. There was the revelation that the Russians possessed the atomic bomb—a revelation which created new fear in the minds of those intelligence services who were, in the words of the Hoover *Report*, prone, as is common among the military, to interpret "the capabilities of potential enemies" as "their intentions."[14] The military authorities entrusted with planning the NATO defenses shared the common and understandable dislike of soldiers for mere "token forces," and wanted NATO to measure up to its presumed military as well as its political responsibilities. Then came the Korean War which by a quite unrealistic analogy

---

[14] The Commission on Organization of the Executive Branch of the Government, *Task Force Report on National Security Organization* (January, 1949), p. 76.

was interpreted as the prelude to a similar immediate attempt to reunite Germany by force. Most people in Washington felt that the need for creating an "effective defense force" for western Europe against Soviet aggression had suddenly become urgent, and in deciding upon its form failed to utilize available evidence as to Soviet techniques of expansion, and took a purely external view of Soviet policy. Once this happened it was politically inevitable that the Americans should demand that their allies agree to the inclusion of a German component in the Western forces. Some authorities' contention that this corresponded to "a steady undercurrent of responsible opinion throughout Europe"[15] is hard to sustain in view of the disarray into which the suggestion plunged both the British and French governments. It was in these circumstances, that the French government, naturally keen on the appointment of an American commander for NATO, put forward the European Army idea as a method of arming the Germans while avoiding a revival of the German menace.

This improvisation was originally received with much scepticism at Washington.[16] But it came to make a pronounced appeal to the new Supreme Commander and to his staff. Thus when General Eisenhower became President Eisenhower, and when he chose for his secretary of state a man who was already committed to the idea of an integrated Europe and to that of using American pressure to bring it

---

[15] John J. McCloy, *The Challenge to American Foreign Policy*, p. 29.

[16] See McGeorge Bundy, *The Pattern of Responsibility* (Boston, Houghton Mifflin, 1952), pp. 116 ff.

about, the way was clear for a coming together of administration and congressional opinion. But even when allowances have been made for all these elements which a concentration exclusively on Congress would tend to ignore, it is difficult not to accept the verdict of a German student of these developments that "the history of the problem of European integration within the American Congress is an example of legislative initiative in the field of foreign policy. The American executive only accepted with considerable reluctance the demand of the Legislature to support European integration."[17] The "Pacific pact" idea provided an even clearer example of Congressional initiative. Such inquires leave open the question of whether the specific differences which emerge from time to time are based upon a fundamental and permanent difference of conception as between the two branches of government. One qualified observer writing on the development of American policy in the last year of the Truman administration put it fairly starkly: "The administration had chosen to base American foreign policy for the most part on multilateral courses of action which were designed to promote the interests of this country in concert with those of other friendly nations. Congress, with some notable exceptions, still tended to act upon the older view which conceived this country's interests as separate from, if not actually antagonistic toward, those

---

[17] Hans-Jürgen Steiringer, "Die Auslandshilfsgesetzgebung des amerikanischen Kongresses und die Europäische Integration," *Europa Archiv* (March 20, 1954); Cf. C. C. Walton, "Background for the European Defence Community," *Political Science Quarterly* (January, 1953).

of the outside world."[18] But this again might seem an over-simplification, since in this instance, whatever the practicability of Congress's plan to use American influence to affect shaping of the European political system, it could hardly be described as based on the conception of America's interests as being something apart; on the contrary, it was claimed that it was America's own interest in European stability together with the sacrifices made by America to reinforce it, that gave Americans the right to dictate the institutional forms it should take, if their efforts were to be maintained.

Two comments on this problem might be in order. In the first place, the general tendency of all modern political societies is to centralize power in the executive; and the American president having come to represent in so direct a way the people's choice is in a particularly fortunate position to profit by this fact if he so desires. Indeed a few years ago, a well-informed observer of the American scene could assert that the new media of communication, first fully exploited by President Roosevelt in the fireside chats (and since then reinforced by television) were so important that the President's access to these fully "redressed the past advantage of the Congress" in "the constant battle for the mind of the people."[19] It is not surprising that Congress has fought back and that it has rested its case for equal power on the fact that it represents not some merely generalized national interest, such as the

---

[18] R. P. Stebbins, *The United States in World Affairs, 1952* (New York, Harper and Bros., 1953), p. 56.

[19] See the essay by James Reston in *Public Opinion and Foreign Policy*, ed. Lester Markel, p. 77.

President purports to represent all the time, but can in fact only literally represent in wartime, but rather the whole living nation in all its multiplicity and variety. Congress rightly claims to be the more sensitive mirror of popular feeling; and it uses this claim both in its contest with the President and in defending its policies against foreign critics.

When some members of the Council of Europe met in the autumn of 1951 with a delegation from the United States Congress, they were addressed by Representative Smith in these unequivocal terms: "I might here say that our Economic Cooperation Administration legislation is not the language of Members of Congress; it is the language of the people of the United States, because we merely represent them and we merely do the things they have bid us do." Senator Humphrey called the Mutual Security Act's admonition about European federation "the crystallized desire of the American people."[20] The claim of Congress to be able to crystallize the American people's desires will not lightly be abandoned.

This being so, it is obvious that the American system can only work if the administration and particularly the State Department can arrive at a working partnership with Congress and in particular with its committees—the latter being especially important in dealing with the House where the floor debate is relatively unimportant. The importance attached by the State Department to achieving such a partnership and the growth within it of its department of Congressional relations are familiar features of the postwar Washington scene.

---

[20] *Conference of Strasbourg* (November 19–23, 1951), *Official Record*, pp. 200, 139.

A step initiated by the Department though ostensibly emanating from Congress was the creation of subcommittees of the Foreign Relations and Foreign Affairs committees corresponding to the Department's own internal organization. Nevertheless, however forthcoming the Department and its head may be—and some Secretaries will do better "on the Hill" than others—such a relationship will clearly demand the consistent participation of the President himself. He alone carries the requisite prestige, and he cannot confer it upon any subordinate. Secretary of State Dean Acheson has recently pointed out that this aspect of the presidency is particularly important where foreign policy is concerned because in this field, leadership within Congress is less effective than in others. In the absence of presidential leadership the role of special groups and of immediate electoral considerations is too powerful, he believes, for sound policies to develop.[21]

What executive officers are always hoping for is that Congress should enact general principles and leave them with the details. This was broadly the case with both lend-lease and the Marshall Plan. Sometimes they hope that the technicalities of a program will enable them to do under the guise of detailed administration things which it is unlikely they would ever be able to do if Congress knew more about them.

There is a tendency in Mr. Acheson's argument in favor of presidential leadership—a tendency natural in an administrative officer with his attention concentrated on the end product—to suggest that American foreign policy would

---

[21] Dean Acheson, "The Responsibility for Decision in Foreign Policy," *Yale Review* (Autumn, 1954).

derive more coherence if party ties were stronger and party leadership firmer. This would surely only be the case when the President and the Congressional majority were of the same party, and even then, if the two parties were divided over foreign policy, their alternation in power might simply produce a series of sharp twists, and deny to foreign policy that element of continuity which is usually held up as one of its principal *desiderata*. A British statesman, in a passage already quoted, argued that greater unity between the parties as well as between the President and Congress was desirable from the point of view of America's allies.

On no branch of the whole of our subject is thinking in a more confused state perhaps, than on the role of a democracy's informal institutions, its political parties, in the sphere of foreign policy. It is not always clear to those who argue about this point what has in fact been the normal practice either in the United States or elsewhere. Yet whether or not the political parties within a given country differ about foreign policy is a question of fact and not of morals. Neither partisanship, nor bipartisanship are moral imperatives. Although Britain is frequently pointed to as a country where foreign policy has been left out of party strife, this has not been true historically except intermittently. We know that Whigs in eighteenth-century England drank port in order to confirm the alliance with Portugal, while the Tory adherents of the French connection were permitted to drink claret; there were circles in England not long ago where the drinking of sherry was frowned upon lest the profits on its sale improve the prospects of the Franco regime. These slightly picturesque examples may serve to drive home the general point that where differences over foreign policy exist, and where the distribution of such differences is not arbitrary—as may theoretically be the case—but coincide with other divisions within the society, they will tend to seek an outlet through party channels. And this after all, is what parties are for—to give shape to what are otherwise merely a series of disconnected partialities. Despite the fact that only two elections, those of 1880 and 1935, have been fought over foreign policy, some of the greatest clashes in British political history have in fact related to such question; it is only when, under the rather rigid British two-party system, a minority view cannot get control of either main party—as was true of the pacifist radicals before 1914, or as has been true of the so-called "Bevanites" and of the Tory imperialists since 1945—that one gets the appearance of what Americans call bipartisanship.

Other European countries show the same phenomenon. Even a country with such excellent reasons for maintaining national unity as postwar western Germany has never experienced unanimity where foreign policy is concerned. Indeed the differences between Chancellor Adenauer and the principal opposition party have been as marked over foreign policy as over anything else. In France there has recently been a dramatic revelation of how far certain foreign policies—and in particular the EDC—so far from representing a national consensus, were connected deeply and intimately with the temporary occupation by a single political party of the key position in a multi-party system.

It could be argued that there must be certain restraints on the nature of party warfare over questions of foreign policy which do not apply so emphatically on the domestic scene. But the governing principle is surely the same in both: not to do in opposition what may prove embarrassing when one attains power.

The situation in the United States is less clear, partly because experience in this field has been rather shorter, and because the change in circumstances has made so much of the experience irrelevant. There was a period in the first quarter of a century of America's history when foreign policy was a highly partisan subject; then, except in so far as slavery was involved in issues of continental expansionism, foreign policy was almost removed from the political arena. Over its significance in the last half-century reputable authorities appear to differ.

Lecturing in Oxford in 1952, an eminent American publicist expressed the view that the Democrats had been historically "the party of bold designs," while the Republicans, under whose aegis the heart of the continent had been settled, were the natural party of isolationism. The role of Theodore Roosevelt makes it hard to accept this generalization at its face value; though it helped to put this lecturer on firmer ground when he tried to explain how the Republicans were isolationist towards Europe yet became imperialist when they looked towards Asia.[22] Others have made the difference seem even more fundamentally a question of a geographical concentration of interest.[23] This view would seem to be supported

---

[22] Walter Lippmann, *Public Opinion and Foreign Policy in the United States* (London, Constable, 1952).

[23] Thomas K. Finletter, *Power and Policy*, p. 91.

by the fact that even during the period when the Democratic administration was receiving help from an important element in the Republican party led by Senator Vandenberg, bipartisanship never extended to Far Eastern policy. Senator Vandenberg himself made this plain in a speech to the Senate on March 18, 1947. In fact, he went further and claimed that it had not applied to other policies external to Europe and the United Nations; it had not applied to Latin America for instance, and even on a vital European decision, that to give support to Greece and Turkey, there had been no preliminary consultation with him.[24]

While, therefore, it is undeniable that Republicans have shown themselves more interested in policies in Asia, and have of recent years taken a more belligerent attitude towards the problems of that hemisphere, a good deal must be allowed for the fact that during these years the Republicans as an opposition party could hardly avoid using what appeared to be American errors as a proper topic for party debate. The major weakness of the system here is that once a policy has been made nationally acceptable—nonrecognition of Communist China, for instance—each party may be too afraid of the other to suggest reconsideration of it. It was by no means clear—and after nearly two years of a Republican administration it is not much clearer—that the Republicans, had they been in office from 1944 onwards, would have taken an essentially different view of the priorities in American policy. In the same way one may well wonder whether if on

---

[24] *The Private Papers of Senator Vandenberg* (London, Gollancz, 1952), p. 351.

November 8, 1916, Charles Evans Hughes had in fact woken up to find himself President-elect of the United States, as on the previous evening it had seemed almost certain he would, the subsequent attitude of the two parties towards American participation in a world organization might not have followed a very different course.

What one has to allow for in a system in which active political parties take a prominent part is the likelihood that certain policies will tend to gravitate towards the keeping of one party or another for reasons of a partly ephemeral kind. On issues rather more concrete than the balance between Europe and Asia, the source of a party's electoral support has obviously had its influence also. Indeed Samuel Lubell's thesis that the ethnic origins of a given area's population are still more important than its geographical location for understanding its foreign policy preferences seems to deserve respectful if not uncritical attention.[25] And this element in party calculations is not confined to such historic groupings as Irish-Americans or German-Americans, whose direct influence some current students of the American scene regard as being on the decline.[26] A Democrat will have to be very wedded to the doctrine of containment before openly espousing it in preference to liberation before a Polish-American audience.

Nevertheless, it is probable that although speeches are colored by such factors, national policy is not. It was cus-

---

[25] S. Lubell, *The Future of American Politics* (New York, Harper and Bros., 1952).

[26] See, for example, D. W. Brogan, *Introduction to American Politics* (London, Hamish Hamilton, 1954), pp. 102 ff.

tomary a few years ago when British statesmen found American policy on Palestine highly inconvenient, to discount much of its expression as a mere surrender to pressure from an important element in the New York electorate. This British view seemed not altogether well-founded at the time, though it was shared for instance by the then U. S. Secretary of the Navy.[27] And the fact that United States policy later moved so much closer to the course favored by Mr. Forrestal, without any obvious electoral consequences, may justify this earlier scepticism.

Indeed when one looks at what has actually been done in the field of foreign policy rather than at speeches and resolutions, one is driven if one follows the path of national origins to what can only be regarded as the paradoxical view that what counts is what a student of American politics has recently called the " 'English vote,' formed of some 80,000,000 people who today trace their descent back to the British Isles." Since he argues England has been involved in all the international crises of the present century, "the English-American, reacting in the exact manner of any ethnic strain, has demanded and won support for the 'mother country'."[28] From this point it only seems a step to the statement made by an eminent historian of American diplomacy as the opening sentence of a recent book: "the main objective in American foreign policy since 1900 has been the preservation of the

---

[27] See W. Millis, ed., *The Forrestal Diaries* (New York, Viking, 1951).

[28] Sidney Hyman, *The American President* (New York, Harper and Bros., 1954), pp. 38–9.

British Empire."[29] Surveying the tenacity of the anti-colonialism motif in American foreign policy—its grip for instance on the mind of Franklin D. Roosevelt—a British historian is likely to find this thesis rather implausible.

Whatever weaknesses may exist in the structure of the central organs of the federal executive, and however weak the binding ties of party by European standards, in the working out of national policy, such secondary influences, where they do not cancel one another out, need not then perhaps be viewed too tragically. Their actual effect is simply to add some more colours to the already sufficiently variegated spectrum of Congressional opinion. And even here one should be careful not to overestimate their significance.

If one looks at the list of resolutions presented to the House of Representatives during the Eighty-third Congress one cannot fail to be impressed by the wide-ranging interests of the members who presented them: the bulk of them express resentment at this or that policy of the Soviet Union or its satellites; many recommend the breaking off of diplomatic relations with one or other of the governments concerned; in another vein are a series favoring the unity of Ireland under the Dublin government; neither the one series nor the other were taken any distance in the legislative process; nor is it likely that their sponsors expected anything to happen; for them it was a cheap and easy way of satisfying their constituents.[30] The only danger might be that foreign govern-

---

[29] C. C. Tansill, *Back Door to War* (Chicago, Regnery, 1952), p. 3.

[30] See Committee on Foreign Affairs, *Legislative Calendar*, House of Representatives, 83rd Congress, 1st sess., September 20, 1954.

ments would fail to see it quite that way; but this is a risk inherent in the democratic system.

In such a context bipartisanship reveals itself as simply one more aspect of the executive-legislative relationship. Insofar as Congressional support is necessary for the execution of the Administration's policies, majorities must be found; in a system of this kind, such majorities are likely to be bipartisan to some extent, and from the point of view of continuity it is desirable that they should be. The still inchoate nature of the American parties themselves must be kept in mind; an American student of the problem has pointed out that Republican leadership in Congress has tended to come from the "isolationist" interior. The party's presidential candidates tend to be those favored by the marginal states of the "internationalist" East.[31] This does not mean that the relationship is a static one; indeed at this point in the system more than at any other, the element of personality is perhaps all-important. One challenge may come from a difference of opinion over where certain rights of decision are constitutionally located; the so-called great debate of 1951 over the reinforcement of American troops in Europe under the NATO treaty ended without any clear definition of the extent of the President's prerogatives as commander-in-chief.

The existence of this constitutional no-man's land may tempt military personalities whose views differ from those of the President Commander-in-Chief to seek to use Congres-

---

[31] H. B. Westerfield, "Opinions et partis dans la politique étrangère Américaine contemporaine," *La Politique Etrangère et ses Fondements*, p. 132.

sional support to get their own way. The fact that the armed services have traditionally been obliged to lobby for their own appropriations makes such action less striking perhaps than it would be under a tighter system, such as the British one. President Roosevelt's preference for by-passing the civilian heads of the service departments and for dealing direct with uniformed officers also contributed to the new importance of the military as a factor in policy-making. Nor can civilian leaders make too much fuss about military encroachments on their responsibilities, so long as they tend to exploit the popularity of military figures with Congress by pushing them forward as their major advocates even on the nonmilitary aspects of their international programs. It is nevertheless striking for the foreign student brought up on the classical view of the United States as the most civilian-minded of the great powers, to observe the ultimately indecisive nature of the other great debate of 1951, that over the recall of General MacArthur.[32] In a sense, of course, it was not indecisive, in that when it came the point the policies which he had objected to were in fact confirmed; but it is obvious from the subsequent conduct and writings of his supporters, that the issue was still thought of by them in terms of rival military-political strategies and that the issue of civilian control which had seemed paramount to President Truman and his advisers both civil and military was never taken seriously at all.

I think it is not going too far to say that given the nature

---

[32] R. P. Stebbins, *The United States in World Affairs, 1951*, pp. 49–56, 98 ff. Cf. R. H. Rovere and A. M. Schlesinger, Jr., *The General and the President* (New York, Harper and Bros., 1951).

of modern arms and modern warfare, the major institutional aspect of the whole problem of democratic foreign policy has come to be that of the relations between the civilian and military components of government. A learned study of the problem by an American scholar, completed just before the events of 1951, ended with a reaffirmation of the view that, despite weaknesses, the system established by the Founding Fathers was still "adequate for the needs of the United States in peace and war."[33] It is not for a foreigner to call such a judgment into question; but there is one aspect of the foreign policy problem which I have only touched in passing but which has a direct relevance to this theme of civilian control, though its ramifications are much wider.

We have seen already that one of the tasks of the makers of foreign policy is to define national interest, and that another is to bring about a proper relationship between the policies this interest would seem to demand, and the realities of national power. But in order that this can be done effectively, a third element enters in: that of the power and policies of other states. Such distinctions are again artificial; the power and policies of other countries are continually being affected by the actions of one's own country, quite apart from their inherent capacity for change. Nevertheless there is a sense in which objective information about other countries—about their power, their institutions, their outlook and their policies —is crucial to any attempt at policy-making. It is not clear that democracies normally appreciate the significance of this

---

[33] Louis Smith, *American Democracy and Military Power* (Chicago University Press, 1951), p. 324.

factor (it is indeed the point at which the expert and the layman most often part company) and it is probable that their institutions are often ill designed to give it proper weight. The tendency to make information serve policy, not policy rest upon information is an inevitable one.

I suspect that the military mind rightly trained to make decisions in the field on the basis of intelligence that must be imperfect in most cases, is particularly prone to underestimate the complexity of the task involved in making decisions where a political as well as a military element is involved.

A classic American instance might be provided by General MacArthur's reluctance to admit that a calculation of Soviet intentions in Europe was relevant to the decision as to how the war in Korea was to be fought.[34] But where proper civilian guidance is lacking, the military may have no alternative but to step in. One example of this seems to have been the failure to consider the political aspects of the Japanese situation in the summer of 1945, and the concentration upon purely military means of bringing about a surrender. What appeared to be a War Department assumption of authority for settling vital policy in the early stages of the occupation of both Japan and Germany was unavoidable because no coherent policy for these countries had been worked out in the State Department after the fiasco of the "Morgenthau plan" for Germany. Furthermore the actual chiefs of occupation forces are almost certain to be able to make policy on a considerable scale by their day-to-day decisions. Neither General Mac-

---

[34] R. P. Stebbins, *The United States in World Affairs, 1951*, pp. 106–109.

Arthur nor General Lucius Clay were seriously subjected to control from Washington.

If this primacy of the military takes place in a situation where there is a potential enemy, its dangers are obvious enough even if one dismisses as an intellectual's myth the idea that soldiers are more bellicose than civilians, and recognizes the fact that most great American soldiers have been firmly devoted to the principle of civilian control. "The military planner," it has been authoritatively pointed out, "has to act on what he calls assumptions. . . . Obviously the assumptions are the controlling thing. One weakness of our present military planning is that the foreign policy men in the government do not take enough part in the making of these assumptions."[35] This may be still more serious if plans are based upon military intelligence which is itself faulty. After the failure directly to predict the North Korean attack in 1950, the intelligence authorities apparently became so cautious that they seemingly suggested the likelihood of further attacks at almost every point on the periphery of the Communist world. Against a danger so generalized no serious political or military planning was possible.

This does not mean that civilian experts are infallible. Their frame of reference may also be too narrow for the job. A scholarly writer has examined, for instance, the much debated question of why the United States government received from some of its representatives in wartime China an erroneous impression of the nature and aims of the Communist movement there. His conclusion attaches great importance—

---

[35] Thomas K. Finletter, *Power and Policy*, p. 324.

I am sure correctly—to the fact that "almost none of the government officials" who conducted "relations with China day by day were well-schooled about either Communist dogma or methods. Their training and experience were predominantly in the Oriental countries and the Oriental languages. . . . Few had felt the need to make a thorough study of the history and tactics of Communism, and fewer still had pondered deeply over its secret inner nature and compulsions." Ambassador Patrick Hurley's own independent view that the Chinese Communists were not really communists at all was also that of someone without the basic training for making judgments of this kind.[36]

But to say that observers should be better schooled is not to solve the whole problem in a field in which legitimate differences of opinion may emerge. Disagreements on the interpretation of the Chinese scene in the war and immediately postwar years are reminiscent of the differences over the interpretation of events in Russia in 1917–18 between Ambassador Francis on the one hand, and certain members of his staff on the other. It is likely to be the dominant view in official circles that all is well so long as information and views are channeled through the head of the mission and it may have been applicable to some situations in the past, and the case is enhanced where actual operations are concerned. But there is the question of what happens if the head of the mission in question is unwilling to pass on information that conflicts with the assumptions on which official policy is based, or if the head of the mission himself knows that he will be overborne by some super-ambassador on special mission whom the

---

[36] Herbert Feis, *The China Tangle*, p. 184.

secretary of state of the day regards as a more direct exponent of his policies. These questions were raised in the minds of European observers by the attitude of the State Department in 1954 to the prospect that the EDC treaty would be ratified by the French National Assembly. They were tempted to wonder whether the reputed instructions to the Policy Planning Staff not to consider alternatives if the French should fail to ratify, were not extended to make difficulties in the way of those who sought to report what was obvious enough to anyone outside American governmental circles, namely that ratification of the treaty in its original form had long been out of the question.

These things cannot be known in full until the archives are open; but it is obvious that the chance of such things happening, that is to say of United States policy being based upon misleading information about other countries, is much enhanced by the recent tendency in Congress and the public to regard as culpable, even as treasonable, mistakes which were made in perfect good faith. As we read in a new study of the presidency: "if the men in the field were to write full, frank and critical reports, they had to be reasonably certain that they were writing in confidence for the eyes of their superiors alone. That confidence was shaken when supposedly confidential reports were broadcast after Congressional hearings, when simple statements of fact were wrenched out of a context and used to support demands for a loyalty investigation."[37] The point was made by this author to explain the

---

[37] Sidney Hyman, *The American President*, p. 297. Cf. Henry M. Wriston, "Young Men and the Foreign Service," *Foreign Affairs* (October, 1954).

weakening of civilian as opposed to military influence in the counsels of government. But if it becomes impossible for a government to rely on its servants giving it objective information irrespective of whether or not the information is palatable, the damage may go much further and indeed prove fatal. Curiously enough, a standard work written in 1950, while having much of interest to say on the co-ordination of intelligence and the need for an historical background for its evaluation, did not touch on this fundamental question.[38]

My own impression is that the particular kind of naivete displayed a few years ago by those American public servants who were the main subsequent target of Congressional wrath is unlikely to recur. The foreign visitor to American institutions of learning cannot help being impressed by the enormous effort being put into the scholarly study of the foreign scene, and in particular of the Soviet scene. Through their publications alone such institutions as the Russian Institute of Columbia University, or the Harvard Russian Research Center have put the whole non-Soviet world deeply in their debt.[39] Even more important is the contribution which has been made to the nation's resources in the training of specialists well equipped to deal with the many different sides of the United States' relations with the Soviet Union. We must therefore assume that the relevant departments of the United States government including its service departments will increasingly

---

[38] J. L. McCamy, *The Administration of American Foreign Affairs*, Chap. XIII.

[39] See, for example, L. G. Cowan and G. T. Robinson, *History of the Russian Institute, Columbia University* (New York, Columbia University Press, 1954).

be staffed by personnel of the highest competence in this field. Nevertheless one has an uneasy feeling that much of this *expertise* will be left unused so long as quite unqualified publicists are prepared to supply views and interpretations of the Soviet scene which fit better into the modes of thought and instinctive prejudices of their audiences; I have already indicated my belief that *expertise* on the Soviet Union was ignored in the vital decision of 1950. The task of interpreting foreign countries is never as straightforward as the nonexpert often thinks. The fact that the Policy Planning Staff of the State Department, despite the contrary recommendation of the Hoover Commission, has come to be used almost exclusively on current business suggests that the nature of the problem is still largely unappreciated.

I have heard it argued that the United States can afford weaknesses in its official supply of information from abroad because its newspaper correspondents are so excellent. It would certainly be unbecoming to disparage their contribution. But it is not altogether the case that newspaper correspondents abroad are totally independent of the official line where this is very strongly marked. A letter to the *New York Times* printed in that paper on September 18, 1954 said that because of the almost unanimous support for EDC in the United States there had been no healthy debate on the subject at all, and that the depth and complexity of French opposition to it had never been properly explained to the American people who were encouraged to believe that only "Communists, Fascists and chauvinists" were opposing the treaty.[40]

---

[40] Letter from Frederick Wallach of Bayside, New York.

If this state of things is rare, there is no question but that certain newspapers may act as an accelerator rather than a brake in the pursuit of an ill-founded course of policy. After the sustained *mea culpa* of the last volume of the official history of the London *Times*, there can be no doubt but that all news from Germany or elsewhere which might conflict with the belief that a settlement with Hitler was possible was resolutely pushed into the background.[41] Editorial policy governed news policy. Indeed if anything, the official history is too reticent; it does not go into the *Times* own private gesture of appeasement: the sacrifice to Nazi animosities of an excellent Berlin correspondent; nor does it tell the story, for which we have had to await the Duff Cooper memoirs, of the distortion of its own lobby correspondent's account of the scene in the Commons on the occasion of Duff Cooper's resignation after Munich.[42] Newspapers have their valued place in a democratic society; but they cannot substitute for government.

This problem of information is of special concern to senators and congressmen, and if their thirst for information through Committee hearings is bound to be unpalatable to busy officials, it does represent at least one way in which information can be conveyed where it is most needed, while at the same time contributing something to the wider education of the public. Unless one is to take a totally cynical view of

---

[41] *The History of the Times,* Vol. IV (London, The Times, 1952), Part 2, Chap. XXIII.

[42] Duff Cooper (Viscount Norwich), *Old Men Forget* (London, Hart-Davis, 1954), p. 251.

the travels undertaken by American legislators in these post-war years, one must assume that the problem of acquiring adequate information is one of which they are very conscious. But the task is almost an impossible one for men who have a great many other responsibilities. Despite the work put in by the committee staffs and the legislative reference service of the Library of Congress—two aspects of Congress that any European legislature must profoundly envy—the maximum they can hope to achieve is a better capacity for judging the information which the administration offers in defense of its policies, and as support for its demands. It is perhaps unlikely that future legislators will show the same arrogant confidence in the superiority of their own sources of information as was shown by Senator Borah on a famous occasion in 1939.[43] In a more sophisticated age, the Senate is unlikely to rejoice in that innocence of geography which caused that body to suggest as a solution for the transcaucasian problem during the Russian Civil War that an American battleship might be sent to Baku.[44] But how far a determination to get the facts right first is likely to make progress in Congress remains uncertain; and this must be still truer of the general public, which is under even less pressure in this respect.

For it is not only a question of the facts of the current situation in the narrower sense; there is the further problem that for their interpretation, a long historical perspective is

---

[43] W. L. Langer and S. Everett Gleason, *The Challenge to Isolation (1937–1940)* (New York, Harper and Bros., 1952), pp. 143–45.

[44] See Firuz Kazemzadeh, *The Struggle for Transcaucasia, 1917–1921* (Oxford, George Ronald, 1951), p. 262.

often essential. Americans may regret that Europeans seem so enmeshed in the web of their own history, and the former tend to assume that the slate was a clean one at the precise moment when they arrived to write on it. The trouble is that the history is itself part of the facts; and not only other people's history. It has recently been shown how the protagonists of Atlantic solidarity in the Second World War gave quite misleading accounts of President Wilson's reasons for intervening in the first.[45] Experience suggests that one's own history may be particularly hard to grasp when it is a question of analyzing decisions that seem to have gone wrong. It then seems natural to talk as though the decisions taken in the past could have been taken in the light of what was later known to be the truth.

What the public mind largely acts upon in foreign policy is a series of myths about the past—myths which indulge democracies in the fallacy that the right course is always ascertainable and practicable. Above all, it is the larger factors in the situation that may get overlooked. How much controversy might have been saved and how many deep divergences in the nation avoided, if Americans had remembered constantly three simple facts: that in the closing years of the war against Germany what the Western Allies most feared was a separate peace by the Russians; that the Far Eastern discussions at the Yalta conference were dominated by the belief that appalling American casualties could only be avoided if Russia came into the Far Eastern war early enough to

---

[45] Robert Endicott Osgood, *Ideals and Self-Interest in America's Foreign Relations*, pp. 111 ff.

make an invasion of the Japanese home islands unnecessary; that the major source of Soviet strength in postwar Europe in the first crucial years was the absolute determination of the American people to see its armed forces demobilized at the maximum speed. Yet, this is no case of the necessary documents being unavailable for the historian; each of these three points can be documented from sources at which no critic could cavil. Yet each of the three has been consistently and pointedly ignored by the myth-makers and treason-seekers.

Nor has it been easy to convince them of their errors. The hearings before the Senate Foreign Relations Committee on the nomination of Charles Bohlen to the American Embassy in Moscow produced on the part of Senator Ferguson a blank refusal to admit that judgments proved wrong in the light of facts unknown at the time—the potentialities of the atom bomb in this case—could be justified as perfectly consonant with what was then known.[46] It was on this occasion that Mr. Bohlen, in replying, made an invaluable addition to the vocabulary of historical criticism.

Looking back on these wartime conferences with the advantage of ten years' experience of their sequels, one had, he admitted, the advantages of hindsight; he continued: "I might also add the advantages of hindmyopia, because the terrific compulsions of the war are absent when you look at it ten years afterwards." There appears to be no institutional solution to the democratic disease of hindmyopia.

---

[46] "Nomination of Charles E. Bohlen," Hearings before the Committee on Foreign Relations of the U. S. Senate, 83rd Congress, 1st sess.

IV *The New Dimensions*
OF FOREIGN POLICY

I T WOULD PROBABLY BE WRONG TO SUGGEST THAT
the kind of problem that confronts a government in the field
of foreign policy is wholly different when that government
happens to be what we usually style democratic. The charges
that Tocqueville levels against democratic governments, their
lack of perseverance, of necessary secrecy and of patience,
could all be made against governments of a different inspiration. Napoleon III for instance compares unfavorably with
many of his democratic successors; and Mussolini with some
of his democratic predecessors. One finds prevalent in many
quarters today the curious illusion that modern totalitarian
governments—that of Soviet Russia for instance—do not
suffer from the disabilities of democracies. But the record of
Soviet diplomacy shows an inability to distinguish between
the real and the imaginary, a series of false calculations
about the capabilities and intentions of foreign countries, and
a record of clumsy coordination between diplomacy and
propaganda which could hardly be improved upon by the
government of any other great state in recent times.[1]

We should not be surprised to find that this is the case.
For if it is right to assume that the most important need in
foreign policy is the ability correctly to calculate the ratios
of power, then a regime wedded to a particular ideology and
limiting its observations by the prescriptions of that ideology
is peculiarly ill suited for the task. The empiricism that the

---

[1] I have argued the case for this view in my books *The Foreign
Policy of Soviet Russia, 1929–1941* (London, Oxford, 1947,49), 2
vols.; and *Soviet Policy in the Far East* (London, Oxford, 1953).

Russian leaders have shown in dealing with internal problems may well have no parallel in the external field where orthodox Marxism-Leninism retains its sway over their minds. Indeed, the problem of understanding correctly the process of secular change is a perennial one. A British student of nineteenth-century Europe has recently emphasized, that for two generations after 1815, the strength of France was consistently overestimated by all the European powers, democratic and undemocratic alike.[2] Most American students of present-day Europe tend to believe that French and British fears of German rearmament are based upon an exaggerated view of what German power is now capable of doing. Clarity of thought in matters so vital to one's own national existence may be out of the reach of any government. All statesmanship in foreign affairs is certain to be imperfect; democracy may make its task harder in some respects, while making it easier in others. What can be said is that democracies do not always make the most of their counterbalancing advantages. For instance, the greater freedom of movement and the liberty of contacts they allow their citizens should add up to a better understanding of the world outside their borders than a totalitarian government can hope for; if as a part of their defense against totalitarianism they impose fetters upon the free movement of their own citizens or upon their contacts with hostile communities, the greater part of the loss is likely to rebound upon themselves. Sometimes they act consciously in their own despite because of exaggerated fear; at other times, it may be due to

---

[2] See A. J. P. Taylor, *The Struggle for Mastery in Europe, 1848–1918, passim.*

a fundamental lack of understanding of the effects of their own procedures.

At the Strasbourg Conference with the Council of Europe, in 1951, one member of the House of Representatives, in presenting the American view that European integration was proceeding too slowly, complained that over a relatively small area so many different languages were still spoken and also that passports were needed at each successive frontier. A European might have replied to the former complaint with some expression of regret that at a time when the United States has so decisively entered the world scene, the teaching of foreign languages should seemingly be in retreat all along the line in its system of secondary and higher education, in favor of subjects of less obvious practical or cultural value. And on the second point, when the Congressman declared that he had to answer a thousand questions before he was issued with a passport for the journey to Strasbourg, one could have made clear to him that it was his own government that imposed these formalities upon him; not the governments of the countries he was proposing to visit. On the contrary, an Englishman can travel without a visa from the North Cape to Naples; it is only when he wishes to visit the United States that he becomes aware that such a thing as a visa exists, or that anyone classes him with delinquents by demanding that he have his fingerprints taken.

These are trifles; but with their useful reminder that one of the basic problems in foreign relations is the inability to see one's own country from an external viewpoint, they will serve to introduce the final element in our inquiry. So far we have been assuming that the problems of international relations at the present time are not altogether different from those of the recent past. We have felt able to call upon the historical experience of at least two centuries for guidance. But can we be certain that this assumption is justified, and if not, what are its consequences for our theme?

There are two new factors which must be taken into account at this stage—factors not entirely disconnected but still capable of separate assessment. The first is obviously the unparalleled increase in the destructive power of the weapons of war. This subject, even in its effects upon diplomacy, does not appear to be one upon which the diplomatic historian is likely to throw much light. To say anything useful would demand a knowledge of the theoretical possibilities of such weapons and of conceivable methods of defense against them which only the scientist and the military technician can possess, and from which the general educated public is of necessity debarred, both because of its lack of scientific knowledge and because of the secrecy which the whole subject imposes even in a democracy. There has been much criticism of the intrusion by atomic scientists into the field of policy-making, particularly in the United States.[3] Like the parallel intrusion of service opinion, it seems to be a test which the country's institutions have got to face. Policy-making cannot be reserved to the ignorant; which is not to say that final political responsibility need rest with the expert.

What one can assume is that the knowledge that all-out war would almost certainly mean the annihilation of organized

---

[3] The appearance of such a journal as the *Bulletin of the Atomic Scientists* is highly significant in this respect.

society of the country initiating it, as well as of that of its enemies, and that indeed the whole of civilization, precariously poised as it is on a delicate fabric woven of technical, commercial and administrative strands, might fail to stand the shock, must enter into the calculations of modern statesmen as a deterrent to war in a way in which the limited horrors of "conventional war" could not. Indeed, one feels that some decisions of recent years can only be fully explained on the assumption that this deterrent has already operated. Contemporary foreign policies cannot incorporate the ultimate sanction of war with comparable freedom to that enjoyed by the great powers of earlier ages. To base calculations of the way in which states are likely to behave upon their actions at earlier dates, or even less reasonably upon ideologies formulated in earlier times, is either to ignore the obvious, or else to assume that human nature has altered as rapidly as man's technical capacities have progressed, and that the prudential restraints that have led men to seek their own preservation, and by the extension of this, the preservation of their own societies and ways of life, have suddenly ceased to exist. Warrant for such beliefs might be found, perhaps, in the final frenzies of the inner Nazi leadership; it seems inadequate evidence for the conclusions one would want to build upon it.

The difficulty is that if one believes that this sanction of total war is at least obsolescent, one then enters a twilight world of conflicts of which the techniques have not yet had a long enough permit run to permit the elaboration of a theory about them. We have learned to call it the "cold war"; but for so complex a phenomenon the phrase is too negative.

102

To go further is to speculate; it is safer to turn to the other factor in our new dimensions. So far, we have followed the practice of diplomatic historians in assuming that the nation-state or multinational-empire, the area owing allegiance to a single government, is the effective unit in international relations. And some students would assert that this is adequate even for our thinking about the present and the immediate future. They would see the last three centuries as a period in which the state has steadily strengthened itself as the focus of human loyalties and in its coercive functions.[4] And they would project the process into the future.

So thoughtful a writer as Professor Osgood is quite clear on this point: "The most important reality of international politics is that fact that nation-states are the major units of political life, which command the supreme loyalty and affection of the great mass of individuals in the civilized world. More than ever, since the rise of modern nations several centuries ago, the great mass of citizens feel that their personal welfare, both spiritually and materially, depends absolutely upon the welfare of the nation to which they owe allegiance; and this is true regardless of divergent views about the proper scope of state intervention in private affairs. This situation is not immutable, but neither is it likely to change in the foreseeable future, for such major transformations in man's outlook occur only in the course of centuries."[5]

---

[4] I have traced the earlier growth of the process in my book *The Age of Absolutism, 1660–1815* (London, Hutchinson, 1954).

[5] Robert Endicott Osgood, *Ideals and Self-Interest in America's Foreign Relations*, pp. 10–11.

Such views would be strengthened rather than weakened by a study of the attempts at supra-national organization over the period since the First World War.[6] Both the League and the United Nations have worked successfully where they have been able to enlist for their own purposes the support of major political communities working through their own governments, and have failed notably on all occasions where an attempt has been made to substitute for these allegiances and ties some allegedly higher ideal. Furthermore, except where the sanction of superior force has been readily available, and ruthlessly applied, the whole tendency has latterly been towards creating new political units out of old multinational agglomerations rather than the reverse. The British Commonwealth the most enduring example of international cooperation has functioned only through the process of continuous consultation and has made no headway with the creation of objectives separate from and external to its independent nations.[7] This has not been true only of the "New" Dominions; it has been equally true of so British a country as Australia, and even in wartime. Sovereignty has been fundamental.

Sir Winston Churchill has given in an account of his efforts

---

[6] Cf. my article, "Problems of International Government," *Year Book of World Affairs*, G. Schwarzenberger, ed. (London, Stevens, 1954).

[7] See volumes by Sir Keith Hancock and N. Mansergh, *Survey of British Commonwealth Affairs* (London, Oxford University Press for Royal Institute of International Affairs, 1937–1952); and N. Mansergh, ed., *Speeches and Documents on British Commonwealth Affairs, 1931–1952* (London, Oxford, 1953).

to persuade the successive Australian prime ministers in the summer and autumn of 1941 to leave the Australian division in Tobruk as desired by the Commander-in-Chief in the Middle East, General Auchinleck.[8] He implies that Mr. Fadden's refusal and his insistence on regrouping the Australian forces under a single command was due to political pressure and to his government's vulnerability in the face of an opposition, parts of which he felt were "isolationist in outlook." He faced a renewed refusal to leave the division at Tobruk from the Labour leader Mr. Curtin when the latter became Prime Minister himself. An Australian historian of these events deprecates a political explanation of the episode and points out that all three Australian prime ministers concerned, Mr. Menzies, Mr. Fadden and Mr. Curtin, were simply acting on the military assessment of their own commander, General Blamey, based on his view of the state of the Australian division itself, and of the desirability of concentrating all the Australian forces overseas under their own commander directly responsible to the Dominion government. Such a concentration was, in Mr. Fadden's view, "fundamental to the effective cooperation of Dominion Forces in Empire Armies." The military historian must be the judge of this; the political historian will attach greater weight to Mr. Fadden's other reason for insisting on his point: that it was "vital to the Australian people's conception of the direction and control of its military forces."[9]

---

[8] Sir Winston Churchill, *The Grand Alliance* (London, Cassell, 1950), pp. 367 ff.

[9] Paul Hasluck, *The Government and the People*, Appendix 10.

To the British student of international relations, Commonwealth experience must bulk large. On the other hand, he is bound to recognize that many people both in Europe and in the United States take the view, or seem to take the view, that modern technology and the mass market that it demands, together with the new elements in the military situation have rendered the nation-state a virtually obsolete form of political community. Senator Humphrey told the Strasbourg Conference that he thought it was "about time we struck down the idea of the divine right of the nation state to destroy and suffocate itself." Senator Hendrickson made a statement to the effect that twenty-seven Senators were on record as supporting former Supreme Court Justice Owen Roberts' plan for a convention to draw up plans for a federal constitution of an Atlantic Union. And a House member of the delegation declared that even this was insufficient and that "practical plans for a World Government" should be the "ultimate goal."[10]

Such language could certainly be paralleled in non-Congressional circles. One is left with the task of trying to reconcile it with what appear to be other and equally fundamental attitudes on the part of the American people and of deriving what lessons one can from this confrontation.

It is not difficult to see how America's own experience should have engendered a general prejudice in favor of larger political units and of the federal form of organization, nor why American opinion should have come to believe in the value of a closer union of the west European countries. Such schemes

---

[10] *Strasbourg Conference*, pp. 73, 77–79, 236.

attracted both those who hoped to continue a close relationship between the two halves of an Atlantic community and those who thought that in this way the need for American aid would be lessened, and Americans be able to withdraw at least partially into the isolation which they still preferred. In this double and indeed contradictory appeal the idea of European union was equally fortunate in Europe itself. Some held that it would strengthen the collective resistance to an assumed Soviet threat; others on the contrary, believing that European dependence on America was in part a cause of the existence of such a threat, welcomed the idea because they thought that Europe could thereby recover its independence and its power to negotiate with both world powers in pursuit of presumed objectives of its own. Some thought that European union would reinforce bipolarity; others that it would destroy it.

More difficult was the question of what measures the United States could legitimately take in this respect without sacrificing its allegiance to its democratic process as a universalist ideal. What measures on its part would be desirable, if it were assumed that only a union based on consent could function effectively? This is only the reappearance of a familiar problem in a new guise. The possibility of influencing the course of political development in foreign countries without positively assuming political responsibilities is one that has presented itself more than once to American statesmanship in recent years.

The most dramatic case was of course that of postwar China. We find a report of October 22, 1945, from so authoritative a source as SWNCC (State-War-Navy Co-ordinating Committee) laying down conditions for American aid: "The extent to which political stability is being achieved in China under a unified fully representative government is regarded by the United States as a basic consideration which will at all times govern the furnishing of economic, military, or other assistance to that nation."[11] Since on the one side there existed at that time a movement implacably wedded to the Communist ideology, and on the other a government which consisted in General Joseph Stilwell's picturesque language of "a structure based on fear and favor in the hands of an ignorant, arbitrary and stubborn man,"[12] the objective set was unattainable, and the conditions for aid inapplicable. General Marshall's mission was consequently a foredoomed attempt to square the circle.

It would be more than misleading to insinuate a European parallel here. All one can say is that the disappointment over EDC was due in part to a serious omission in American thinking. Whereas it was understood that American policies could only be made domestically through effective popular support elicited by constitutional processes, in Europe it was thought to be sufficient to make bargains with existing governments. There is no reason to assume that the congressmen who pressed the view that aid should be made conditional on Europe's progress towards integration were unrepresentative of public opinion at home. When Senator Humphrey told the

---

[11] SWNCC Document No. 83/6, quoted by Herbert Feis, *The China Tangle*, p. 375.

[12] T. H. White, ed., *The Stilwell Papers* (New York, Sloane, 1948), p. 115.

Strasbourg Conference that there was more and more "an attitude in America on the part of those in public office, and on the part of the constituencies, that some condition must be applied," if aid were to continue, there was no reason to doubt his word.[13] In his book published in the previous year, Mr. John Foster Dulles had put the point even more forcibly: "The hands-off policy," he wrote, "has not succeeded, and we face a choice between exerting pressure to get done what needs to be done and acquiescing in a continuing disunity."[14] Indeed the whole method by which American policy comes to be formulated—the apparatus of committee hearings and floor debates with the accompanying press comment—is admirably designed to see that a policy of this kind does have support at home. All interests are seemingly taken into account—except those of the ultimate executants of such a policy, the foreign peoples concerned; they alone are represented only indirectly, through those Americans who claim to know what they need.

The British view here may be a rather special one; Britain's reasons for resisting pressure to enter a European federation have received public recognition in the United States, though they have not satisfied some European advocates of federation, who still regard the British attitude as one of clinging to a meaningless and outworn sovereignty. "In the eyes of our British friends," remarked Paul Reynaud at the Strasbourg Conference, "first of all comes the House of Commons, and then nothing, and after that, nothing again; and then

---

[13] *Strasbourg Conference*, p. 139.
[14] John Foster Dulles, *War or Peace*, p. 218.

comes God: and the idea of inserting some kind of authority between the House of Commons and the Almighty seems to them something very like sacrilege."[15]

The truth is perhaps less simple. It seems to be increasingly the case that modern societies tend towards interdependence, while their institutions, particularly their representative institutions, are designed for self-sufficiency. This fact lies at the bottom of the much discussed contrast between the "functional" and the "federal" approaches to the problems of western Europe.[16] What is not sufficiently understood in some quarters, is that the functional approach is itself limited by the ultimate determination of existing political communities to keep the final disposal of their affairs in their own hands. Sooner or later, as experience has shown, there comes a point at which a halt will be called to the divesting by governments of what their electors regard as their primary responsibilities. If deception and disillusion are to be avoided, there is a good deal to be said for staying on the tried ground of intergovernmental and interinstitutional co-operation which enables the electorates of the individual countries to feel that their interests are not being sacrificed to the plans of some anonymous and uncontrollable international bureaucracy.

These issues are more clear cut perhaps in a system like the British with a familiar line of responsibility running from the Cabinet through Parliament to the majority in the country; the multiparty systems of some continental countries

---

[15] *Strasbourg Conference*, p. 14.

[16] See A. N. Holcombe, "An American View of European Union," *American Political Science Review* (June, 1953).

tend to obscure them because the ultimate test of electoral opinion cannot normally be made in so direct a fashion. Nor of course do parliaments in which the governmental majority is constantly fluctuating, and constantly requiring adjustment, lend themselves to major debates on fundamental questions. The French Parliament for instance, aside from the general debates on the investiture of new prime ministers, did not discuss the basic questions of foreign policy at all between February, 1952, and November, 1953.[17]

Nevertheless, through a variety of channels both parliamentary and extra-parliamentary, the general attitudes prevalent among the people can make themselves felt even under a system such as that of France. The verdict of a British student of the Third Republic would probably be endorsed by students of the fourth: "Through the operation of the ballot," he wrote, "and the means of indirect pressure that this entails, the majority of the electorate continuously assumes ultimate responsibility for all the actions of the State. The direction of policy changes in accordance with the fluctuations of dominant opinion."[18]

If this is indeed the case, then the apparent postwar enthusiasm in some French quarters for an abnegation of sovereignty could only have meant one of two things. Either, in the name of some higher good—security against aggression

---

[17] Pierre Gerbert, "L'influence de l'opinion publique et des partis sur la politique étrangère en France," *La Politique Etrangère et ses Fondements*, p. 100.

[18] J. E. Howard, *Parliament and Foreign Policy in France* (London, Cresset Press, 1948), p. 161.

or economic betterment—there was a willingness to dispense with democratic controls altogether; or alternatively, it was believed that a new European community was actually emerging which could express itself through new institutions which would themselves replace the older ones as the supreme focus of loyalty.[19] More recent events in France have suggested that such views were at no time held by more than a minority even among the politically active elements of the nation.

Since it could plausibly be argued that the military, political and economic developments of the past fifteen years had demonstrated the inherent weaknesses of the political fragmentation of Europe, it must be assumed that the obstacles to integration lie deep indeed; it is not unreasonable to connect them with what people think of as being involved in living in a democracy. Does not going forward with such international institutions ahead of the development of the sense of belonging to a common community mean not only a loss of control but also a loss of that vital spirit of enterprise to which a sense of community gives birth?

We may perhaps learn more about this question if we turn from Europe to the United States itself. It is always tempting for a country, particularly for a democracy, to generalize into universal principles those attitudes which its own situation most naturally dictates. The most symptomatic contemporary example in the United States is perhaps the popular myth about the so-called veto in the United Nations. The veto is almost always talked of as though it were some-

---

[19] Cf. my article, "The 'Federal Solution' in its Application to Europe, Asia and Africa, *Political Studies* (June, 1953).

thing which had been wantonly introduced into the operations
of the United Nations Organization by the Soviet Union for
the express purpose of making that Organization ineffective.
Yet it is clear enough that none of the great or near-great
powers would ever have assented to the Charter without such
a safeguard, and that if the United States had been able to
command for its policies only a minority of votes equivalent
to that which normally follows the Soviet line, it would have
been driven into using the veto with the same frequency which
it finds so maddening in the Russians.

There is indeed a considerable element of ambiguity in the
attitudes of the United States towards the whole question of
transcending national sovereignty, even in areas where the
passions generated by the Soviet threat do not complicate
the matter. This is not to say, that the position of the United
States is identical with that of the west European countries,
or that of her other partners in NATO. On the contrary,
one feature of the contemporary scene which distinguishes
it most sharply from preceding periods is the large gap between the great powers and the rest. All the countries of the
world with hardly any important exception have been in some
sense dependents in recent years either upon the Soviet Union
or upon the United States. And there can be no useful comparison between the role of patron and that of protege. It is more
natural, and indeed more reasonable, for the United States
to claim sovereign control over the disposal of its surplus in
the instruments of defense, economic or military, than for the
recipients to press their sovereign rights with regard to whatever may be allotted to them. Nevertheless the traffic is not
exclusively one way. Each phase in United States policy has

in fact involved new contacts with foreign governments and peoples, and has added to the administrative machinery required for handling them.

By 1948, nineteen agencies of the American government "were concerned with *all* aspects of foreign relations because they operated only within the limits and directions set by our dealing with the other nations. . . . another group of twenty-three agencies outside the Department of State enforced laws usually designed to regulate the activities of individuals who were acting in foreign relations. . . . Forty-six agencies outside the Department of State . . . were concerned in part in 1948 with continuous economic functions in the field of foreign relations."[20] Almost no important branch of the executive was by then altogether outside the mesh of activities linking the life of the United States with that of foreign communities or international institutions; and the situation has not substantially altered in the intervening period.

Furthermore, many things that look altogether domestic, in the sense that Congress can act regarding them without negotiation with foreign governments—in particular the two great fields of tariffs and immigration—have an effect upon foreign countries which is much more significant than a good deal that is normally classed as being concerned with foreign relations. Australia's problem is thus reproduced on a much greater scale. If the economists are right in asserting that world price-levels (and all that goes with them in the shape of employment and investment patterns) are now ultimately

---

[20] J. L. McCamy, *The Administration of American Foreign Affairs*, pp. 107, 116, 120.

determined by the performance of the United States domestic economy, then it is hard to see how any valid distinction between home and foreign affairs can be made. An ultimate responsibility must then rest on American governmental institutions and, through them, on the American electorate for what happens throughout the world; while this situation may appeal to the convinced internationalists in the United States, the reaction against it is for the moment the more striking.

Even the executive branch of government, which is clearly more likely to be aware of the situation in all its implications, cannot help being influenced by the electorate's greater concern with what appear to be purely internal problems, particularly as these make themselves felt through the political parties. An American writer has recently suggested that President Truman was obliged in 1948 to slacken the administration's concentration on foreign affairs and slow down its armament program because of the challenge on domestic policy represented by the Henry Wallace candidacy in the election of that year. People may even advocate foreign policies designed primarily to strengthen their own party in domestic politics. The same writer believes that the Democrats would have been well advised to spend more money on supporting Chiang Kai-shek, since even if the additional aid had also been wasted, the Republicans would have been deprived of one of their main charges against the administration.[21]

Under the American system, however, it is upon Congress that the pressure for separating the domestic from the for-

---

[21] H. B. Westerfield in *La Politique Etrangère et ses Fondements*, pp. 134, 137.

eign aspects of policy will largely fall; the national interest may currently call for liberal trade policies designed to minimize the need for direct economic aid—it is the individual congressman who will be affected by the particular interests of this or that group of his constituents in some special aspect of protection—and it is the sum of these special interests that will tend to negate the general intention of the executive branch. All this is fairly familiar; but what appears to have developed in recent years is a conviction that these defenses are actually insufficient, that the latitude left to the executive to make agreements may enable some American policies to be determined by the presumed or alleged interests of some wider community of the future. To the student of the attempts at European integration and the obstacles into which they have run, the opposition by Americans to the sacrifice of their own sovereignty should not have come as a surprise. The obsolescence of sovereignty is for most Americans a doctrine for export only; and there are good democratic grounds for their taking this view.

One can indeed state the argument in a more general form. Insofar as the various societies of the modern world tend to develop institutional methods of handling their joint concerns, these will operate in favor of the executive element in governments which will be concerned in the negotiation of the relevant agreements, and the operation of the relevant programs. As a corollary these methods will operate to diminish the powers of the legislatures of the countries concerned and hence to lower the prestige of their legislators. The legislators will be told in one form or another that their primary business is to vote the money; thereafter they cannot expect to have detailed control of it. The criteria of acceptability applied to American government servants, for instance, is not generally held in the rest of the world to be suitable for UNESCO. Yet UNESCO depends in great part upon the same source of funds as do the government departments of the United States; why should Congress surrender its say in the one instance and not in the other? It is a further aggravation when the negotiation of international agreements or the signature of international conventions appears to be a way of circumventing the ordinary processes of law-making. And where you have, as in the United States, a federal system with some legislative powers still competed for by the states, the objections of the central legislature may be powerfully reinforced.

The consistent efforts made by the executive branch to associate Congress with the actual conduct of foreign affairs as well as with the formulation of policy show how aware the departments, and particularly the State Department, have been of the problems presented by such attitudes. Senators and congressmen were associated during the war with the departmental efforts at planning the future peace; senators and congressmen were made members of delegations to the important postwar conferences and have always figured on the United States delegations to the General Assembly in the United Nations. But while this may help to increase congressional awareness of the problems faced, it has clearly not been sufficient to disarm congressional suspicions that the real powers of Congress are meanwhile being whittled away.

The series of proposals for constitutional amendment connected with the name of Senator Bricker, and the public

117

debate upon them in Congress and elsewhere, are highly revealing in this respect.[22] Quite apart from the specific proposals that have been made, the fact that an important section of the American legal profession, and a great variety of national organizations of various kinds, ranging from the Kiwanis International to the National Society, Women Descendants of the Ancient and Honorable Artillery Company, are on record as supporting a constitutional amendment on the making of treaties and executive agreements, and the fact that the Senate came so near to action on the subject in the early months of 1954 obliges the student not to underestimate the pressure behind the strength of the movement.[23]

Originally there seem to have been two main currents of thought involved.[24] There was first of all the normal congressional suspicion of the executive, focussed this time on the question of the power to make executive agreements, and fortified by the persistent legends about the harm done by the Yalta agreement—an agreement which the Senate formally repudiated on March 14, 1952, in connection with its

---

[22] For the case for the Bricker Amendment see Felix Morley, *Treaty Law and the Constitution* (Washington, American Enterprise Association, 1953). But see also Stephen H. Hess, "Behind the Bricker Amendment," *New Leader* (February 1, 1954).

[23] For a list of the organizations supporting the Bricker Amendment see Frank E. Holman, *Primer on "Treaty Law" and the Bricker Amendment* (Seattle, Argus Press, 1954).

[24] On the early legislative history of the proposals see Committee on the Judiciary, *Constitutional Amendment Relative to Treaties and Executive Agreements*, U. S. Senate *Report* No. 412, 83rd Congress, 1st sess.

ratification of the Japanese Peace Treaty.[25] It has been this part of the Bricker proposals that has been most consistently opposed by the Administration. As President Eisenhower put it: "It would so restrict the conduct of foreign affairs that our country could not negotiate the agreements necessary for the handling of our business with the rest of the world. Such an amendment would make it impossible for us to deal effectively with friendly nations for our mutual defense and common interests."[26]

The examples quoted by Senator Bricker in his speech in the Senate on August 4, 1954, and other statements made in support of his general position suggest that the root of the matter was an unwillingness to accept the view that the foreign policies the United States had now adopted involved the "handling of business" with the rest of the world.[27] The concept of mutuality of aid remains fundamentally alien despite Senator Bricker's own denial on an earlier occasion that support for his proposals was "a sign of isolationism or xenophobia."[28]

This becomes still clearer when one looks at another aspect of the proposals, the attempt to invalidate any treaty or agreement which (in the language of the latest version of the

---

[25] R. P. Stebbins and C. W. Baier, eds., *Documents on American Foreign Relations, 1952,* p. 288.

[26] Letter to Senator Knowland, January 25, 1954, *Department of State Bulletin* (February 8, 1954).

[27] On the attitude of Congress cf. R. P. Stebbins, *The United States in World Affairs,* pp. 92 ff.

[28] Speech of February 7, 1952. See R. P. Stebbins and C. W. Baier, eds., *Documents on American Foreign Relations,* 1952, p. 70.

proposals) "conflicts with the Constitution or is not made in pursuance of it." Senator Bricker claimed that the principle of this proposal had been endorsed by the Eisenhower Administration.[29] In fact however, as Mr. Dulles pointed out in reference to an earlier draft, language of this kind would debar the United States from ever abridging the power of Congress to declare war through treaties outlawing war, or from participating in effective measures for the international control of atomic energy or of armaments—controls which could not be effective without affecting the entire constitutional structure.[30] It is worth noting that even action under treaties which have been ratified by the Senate is attacked, where it seems to detract from Congressional power. Thus Senator Bricker has denied Mr. Dulles' view that the ratification of the Rio or NATO treaties enables the President to take action at once if America's allies are attacked, without waiting for a Congressional declaration of war. But such arguments—which are likely to prove academic if the occasion for testing them should ever arrive—are less important from our point of view than the positions taken on some subordinate issues. For instance, Senator Bricker's attack on the NATO Status of Forces Agreement, approved by the Senate on July 15, 1953, involves the view that Americans even when serving abroad and as part of an international force remain wholly exempt from the jurisdiction of foreign governments: "the adoption of an adequate treaty-control amendment will

---

[29] Speech of August 5, 1954.

[30] Statement of April 6, 1953, *Department of State Bulletin* (April 20, 1953).

go very far toward eliminating the discrimination as between State Department diplomats stationed abroad and American soldiers drafted and sent abroad to defend foreign soil."[31] The appeal to prejudice hardly requires underlining.

Language of this kind involves ignoring the benefits which the United States might derive under international agreements—a fact very apparent in the attacks made during the committee hearings on the proposed amendment upon certain reciprocity provisions in standard treaties of friendship, commerce, and navigation. It is closely connected with one of the original impulses behind the movement for an amendment, the desire to prevent any change in domestic laws coming about as the result of a treaty, either through its being self-executing, or because of its being taken as conferring new legislative powers on Congress. Indeed some authorities have regarded the "repeal of *Missouri* v. *Holland*" as being the core of the whole Bricker plan.[32]

Here there has been some shift in the Administration's position. The United States government was, at one time seemingly at least, prepared to go along with the view that the international organizations of the postwar world were not confined in their functions to dealings between states. There was an attitude which suggested that the new organizations had wider duties which involved the internal regimes of member states. If this were so, then clearly domestic law might be affected by the United Nations Charter itself, and

---

[31] Speech of August 5, 1954.

[32] Morris D. Forkosch, "What the Amendment Means," *New Leader* (February 1, 1954).

by conventions reached under its provisions. Indeed the California land case—despite the subsequent reversal of the judgment—was a pointer in this direction.[33] It was this possibility of an actual vast extension of the doctrine of *Missouri v. Holland*, particularly by way of conventions reached under the auspices of bodies like the I.L.O., which were popularly believed to be unsound on major issues of property rights, that provided Senator Bricker with the kind of support that led him to attack what he calls the "new international law" of which the "basic premise" is "that the relationship between citizens of the same government and between the individual and his government are appropriate subjects for negotiations, definition and enforcement in multilateral treaties." The Republican administration took the view, if we may judge by Mr. Dulles' remarks, that on this point the Bricker amendment was superfluous, because the administration had no intention of entering into agreements within the forbidden area. On his appearance before the Senate Committee on the Judiciary on April 6, 1953, Mr. Dulles agreed that there had "developed a tendency to consider treaty making as a way to effectuate reforms, particularly in relation to social matters, and to impose upon our Republic conceptions regarding human rights which may be felt were alien to our traditional concepts." But the concern which had been rightly aroused was safeguard enough. The new Administration was "committed to the exercise of the treaty-making power only within traditional limits," and he gave as evidence of this America's

---

[33] *"Sei Fujii v. State of California* (1952)," *American Journal of International Law* (July, 1952).

decision not to become party to a Human Rights Covenant nor to sign the Convention on the Political Rights of Women.

The supporters of the Bricker amendment remained unconvinced by a mere pledge on policy, which was only binding on a single administration and they continued to seek to limit the treaty-making power by constitutional restrictions. The argument over these proposed restrictions was at the heart of the hard-fought Senate debate; and the restriction appeared in a new form in the text that Senator Bricker pledged himself to introduce into the next Congress: "a treaty or other international agreement shall become effective as internal law in the United States only through legislation valid in the absence of international agreement."[34] This would still be sufficient not only to bring the House of Representatives into action after every such treaty—since no treaty would now be self-executing—but also to require action by all forty-eight states in any case where the treaty involved their reserved powers. On both counts, it seemed improbable that the executive branch of government could accept it.

So rapid a survey of so intricate a controversy may do injustice to the complexity of the legal and constitutional arguments involved. It may however serve the purpose of showing how difficult it is to dislodge the hold which sovereign governments have over their peoples or, alternatively, how remote we are from devising institutions of an international kind that will give democratic electorates the same confidence that their own tried constitutional procedures normally in-

---

[34] U. S. Senate, Joint Resolution 181, 83rd Congress, 2nd sess., Sec. 2.

spire. It is easy to dismiss the arguments in favor of proposals like the Bricker amendment as sheerly obscurantist; in fact, they represent a genuine element in the thought both of the community at large and of many particular interest groups within it. The administrator and the expert may be very conscious of the unreality of the separation between domestic and foreign affairs; there is nevertheless a real distinction here for many people who believe that it is one between areas in which they can have their say, and others in which their voice is largely, or may largely be, ignored. It is certainly not in the United States alone that such reactions to the fact of international interdependence are observable. It is perhaps only the United States that can afford to vocalize them so readily, and simultaneously to apply so critical an attitude to their manifestation in other lands.

It is customary after inquiries of the kind we have been making to conclude by drawing a moral or pronouncing some kind of exhortation. On this occasion, neither would be in order; no moral could easily be discerned from so rapidly shifting a set of events and attitudes; and to exhort would be impertinent in a guest. Certainly, nothing I would want to say would be exclusively or even particularly American in its application. Reinhold Niebuhr has written with impressive sincerity of the "irony of American history."[35] But the gap between desires and abilities in which he sees the root of this irony is no exclusively American phenomenon; it exists in all or almost all modern democracies; and if American experi-

---

[35] Reinhold Niebuhr, *The Irony of American History* (New York, Scribner's, 1952).

ence seems the most striking, it is only because the scale both of the desires and of the abilities is so much greater.

To his insistence upon humility in face of the uncontrollable historical process, I would only like to add one remark, and that addressed to a much narrower audience. These are lectures on diplomatic history; and though I have given myself some latitude in the interpretation of this term, I have tried to keep it constantly in mind. And even if I had not felt obliged to do so by my terms of reference, the subject matter itself would have given me no option. As one explores the subject of democratic foreign policy, one becomes increasingly aware of the relation of the whole problem to our understanding of history and particularly, though not exclusively, of recent history. More than once we have had occasion to come back to the building up of myths in the public mind—myths about the origins of the two World Wars, myths about the decisions which shaped the subsequent periods.[36] The rapidity with which contemporary events move, their own complexity, the volume, raucousness and shapelessness of the commentary that accompanies them from platform and press help to accelerate the production of myths and to ensure a market for them. Confused always, and often fearful, the mind seeks to bring some order out of the chaos of experience; the myths and the slogans which they engender provide one method; the

---

[36] For a brilliant analysis of the development and effect of one myth see R. B. McCallum, *Public Opinion and the Last Peace* (London, Oxford, 1944). Cf. Etienne Mantoux, *The Carthaginian Peace* (London, Oxford, 1945). Light on another myth is cast by R. Bassett, *Democracy and Foreign Policy, A Case History: The Sino-Japanese Dispute, 1931–1933* (London, Longmans, 1952).

125

use of analogy provides another and an even more dangerous one. Nazi aggression, which is one thing, and Soviet "aggression," which is something quite different, are treated as identical phenomena and the assumed lessons learned in dealing, or failing to deal, with the one are urged as infallible recipes for dealing with the other. As we have seen, it is certainly much easier to handle questions in this semiautomatic fashion than to go behind the myths to enquire what the real problems were, what alternatives were open to us, and why we took the paths we did.[37]

These tendencies in the public mind present a challenge to the professional historian. He may ignore the challenge by saying that no event can have its history written until the dust of controversy has settled and time has winnowed the archives to manageable proportions. If he accepts it, however, and deals with his own times, temptations of another kind may still assail him. He must consciously remember that it is part of his professional duty—which should be as meaningful as the Hippocratic oath for a doctor—to probe and inquire into issues which the majority of his fellow citizens regard as closed. It is, it may be remarked in passing, the business of academic communities to see that he retains the freedom to do this even if the product is unpopular. He must in my view go even further than this; he should in his professional capacity do what he can to escape from the trammels of his national environment. A British historian of the contemporary scene must not confine himself to studying events

---

[37] Cf. my article "Historians in a Revolutionary Age," *Foreign Affairs* (January, 1951).

as they impinge upon British policy or as reflected in the British mind; he must try to view them also as they might appear through French eyes, or American eyes, or Indian eyes, or even through Soviet eyes. This form of mental gymnastic is painful to perform and rarely receives applause—to try to think things through from a foreign viewpoint may even be held un-American; nevertheless it is an exercise that needs performing not just once, but over and over again. An historian of foreign policy who merely writes down what everyone knows and is agreed upon, and differentiates himself from the ordinary practical man only by the number and complexity of his footnotes, performs quite inadequately the function for which society supports him. In some places and at some times, society may itself make the task impossible. In Soviet Russia each new twist of policy makes necessary the instant rewriting of all the relevant history. But a society that behaves in this way does so at its peril. The world we live in gives us all too many things to fear; some real, some imaginary and some that are real but are feared for imaginary reasons. At least there is no need to add to their number; surely we do not need also to fear the search for historical truth.

Index